THIS
journal
BELONGS TO:

....

Boost Your Mood. Train Your Mind. Change Your Life.

3 MINUTE *Positivity* JOURNAL

KRISTEN BUTLER

Founder of *Power of Positivity*

HAY HOUSE

HAY HOUSE INDIA

New Delhi • London • Sydney

Carlsbad, California • New York City

First published by: Power of Positivity, LLC
www.powerofpositivity.com

Published in India by: Hay House Publishers India Pvt. Ltd.
Muskaan Complex, Plot No.3, B-2 Vasant Kunj, New Delhi-110 070, India
www.hayhouse.co.in
contact@hayhouse.co.in

Distributed in the United States by: Hay House, Inc.: www.hayhouse.com®

Distributed in Australia by: Hay House Australia Pty. Ltd.: www.hayhouse.com.au

Distributed in the United Kingdom by: Hay House UK, Ltd.: www.hayhouse.co.uk

Cover design: Rupa Limbu and Lilly Penhall • Interior design: Marites Bautista • Interior illustrations: Angelica Medrano

First Hay House India Edition 2023

ISBN: 978-93-88302-76-0

Printed at Thomson Press India Ltd, Faridabad

Contents

"The positive thinker sees the invisible, feels the intangible, and achieves the impossible."

—WINSTON CHURCHILL

Introduction

Welcome! *Hi, I'm Kristen.*

I'm so excited to start this positivity journey with you. Congratulations on deciding to uplevel your mindset with me and move your life forward in a positive direction. We're going to be taking small, subtle steps each day, but it's going to equal huge happiness and reliable results by the end. The next few months are going to be *epic*! Possibly even life changing!

I'm usually rather quiet and humble about my life and achievements, creating content behind the scenes for Power of Positivity. I've never publicly talked about my success and struggles, just short, inspirational bursts here and there on my Instagram. As my life continues to expand, however, I am feeling increasingly inspired to share the tools and mindset strategies that have helped me go from depressed and broke – literally *broken* – to **happy, thriving and whole**. I'd love to share a little glimpse of what I've overcome and created with you, so that you, too, can feel inspired and empowered to follow your wildest dreams.

Once upon a time, I was a happy little Kristen who lived by the adage, "Ignorance is bliss." I knew what I wanted in life and was inspired and determined never to be derailed from that. I had huge goals at a very young age. I had a deep, innate connection with God and nature. I felt the depth of my purpose and vision in my heart, but I had little encouragement. In fact, I allowed outside negativity and discouragement to eat away at me and my BIG dreams little by little.

Over time, staying true to myself became increasingly difficult. I experienced extreme adversity, trauma, and hardship. Without enough positivity tools to release negativity and heal, the burdens literally started to weigh me down. Nevertheless, I ignored the internal signs of stress and fatigue, and I kept pushing forward. I wasn't going to let life slow me down.

> I was proud of myself for how well I "managed" and refused to give up on my dreams.

After a few pivots, grand successes, and devastating failures, I finally hit rock bottom. I wore myself out, and I had nothing more to give – to myself or to others. My life didn't feel like my own anymore. And, it wasn't. I had allowed trauma, people-pleasing, and low self-esteem to lead me into becoming depressed, anxious, overweight, broke, and completely lost. I had pushed myself so far beyond my breaking point that I felt exhausted, and I literally collapsed. I was bedridden for weeks.

Every area of my life was falling apart. I was disappointed in myself. I was *always* a solution-oriented person, but during this dark time, I let my mind fall to becoming a victim. The little confidence I had left in myself and my abilities had disappeared. I felt completely worthless, like I had failed myself and God's vision for my life.

Have you ever felt like this?

Most of us have been there at one time or another. Living becomes about just trying to make it from one day to the next. We feel negative emotions daily – worry, blame, resentment, depression and anxiety, just to name a few. Our life doesn't feel like our own anymore. We feel so stuck that we don't even know how to begin to climb out of the deep hole we fell into or created.

Rock bottom is somewhere none of us ever want to be, but sometimes it happens. It's a place that, if we allow it, can destroy us. On the other hand, it can teach us about the deepest, darkest parts of ourselves for our ultimate *growth*.

Rock bottom can be our greatest teacher – as long as we don't stay there for too long.

Fast forward to today, and my life has made a complete 180° transformation. I am healthy and have released half of my body weight. I beat severe anxiety, panic attacks, and depression without medication. I birthed two beautiful girls after being told I could never have children. I went from bankruptcy to financial abundance, and unemployed to being a successful entrepreneur, doing what I love.

How was I able to make these changes and create a happy life?

I am not better than anyone else. The same energy of creation that flows through me also flows through you. If I can do it, anyone can. In fact, I believe, with all my heart, that anyone can improve and create a life they love from where they are right now.

You couldn't get much lower than I was a decade and a half ago, and now I am inspiring millions around the world with my work. I am living my passion. I am fulfilling my purpose. I am showing up in the world as my authentic self. I am genuinely happy. Of course, I am still growing, learning and transforming. My life has challenges and areas I'd like to overcome and improve, but I am happy and grateful for the journey.

- ✓ **I want YOU to feel like this.**
- ✓ **I want YOU to know that you can have whatever your heart desires.**
- ✓ **I want YOU to be happy, even amidst challenges.**
- ✓ **I want to see YOU happily live the life of your dreams.**

This is why I created this journal.

The content and activities in this journal are intentionally created by me for YOU. They are a culmination of over a decade of research, learning, observation, exploration, and experimentation both in my own life and in the lives of those around me.

I've used these daily concepts to transform my mindset and habits while growing the Power of Positivity brand into a global community with over 50 million followers worldwide.

The content, check-in's, prompts and activities I share with you in this journal are the exact positivity tools I used to transform my life. I needed help, and no one was going to do it for me but me. I am confident that when you commit to doing these daily entries, your life will begin to improve for the better as well.

Journaling is the perfect way to shift your emotions immediately and process your feelings without judgment, so you don't get stuck in unpleasant experiences. I've made it easy for you with the quick, done for you check in's, fun activities, inspiring quotes, and easy-to-follow prompts. All you need to do is show up and do the exercises written in this journal, and you'll become the driver of your own vehicle instead of letting life take over and drive your days.

"Instead of
planning for the
worst-case scenario and
feeding your anxiety,
how about expecting the
best-case scenario and
restoring your peace."

@POSITIVEKRISTEN

There is ancestral magic that happens when your pen hits the paper and science agrees. The synaptic connections for process and memory formation are triggered when you physically write something down. It also helps you to be more aware of your worries and your desires.

I truly believe that you will fall in love with the feeling of *setting up and closing your* day in such a positive way.

When you put in the daily effort to acknowledge your current reality and hold yourself accountable for your own choices, thoughts, and emotions, you will slowly but surely align yourself with who you want to be and where you want to go – this change will drive you there without you exerting any extra effort. Over time, people in your life will notice a drastic change in you and will ask what you're doing differently.

Whether you are going through a tough time right now, need a little boost, extra inspiration or accountability, please know, we're in this together. The Power of Positivity community is here to extend a hand out to you.

I invite you to connect with **@powerofpositivity** on Instagram and with my personal account, **@positivekristen**.

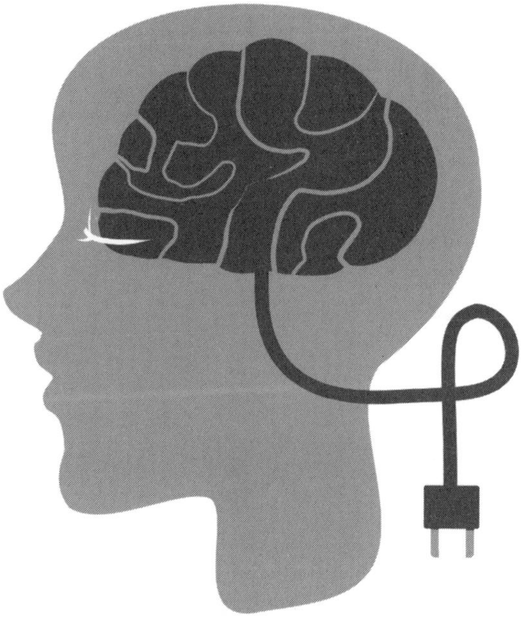

The secret to positivity, training your mind, and improving your life is to make yourself accountable for your actions every single day.

I am a big believer in the power of accountability. With this in mind, I encourage you to share your commitment. As you go through this journey, be sure to post about your progress and a-ha moments, tagging both accounts, and use the hashtag **#positivityjournal**. My team and I will keep a close eye on this hashtag to encourage and celebrate, resharing some of your success stories along the way. I am SO excited to be on this journey with you. Please dive into the next few chapters so you can get the most out of your daily entries!

"We overthink happiness. Keep it simple. There is something good in every moment, find and keep your focus there."

@POSITIVEKRISTEN

Why is Positivity Important?

Good news! Your mindset, happiness, and level of achievement have a lot less to do with your genetics and life circumstances than you might think.

Psychologists from the University of California have discovered that both genetics and life circumstances only account for about 50 percent of a person's happiness and positive attitude. Everything else is in your hands – or rather in your mind's power to perceive its environment and situations.

Studies show that people who foster positivity within themselves are less anxious, more successful, more physically and mentally resilient, and recover from injury or illness faster.

The fact is, choosing a positive attitude and developing positive mental and physical habits are good for our health, our relationships, our careers, and even our income level. Positivity can in time override our genetic predispositions, past traumas, life circumstances, health challenges, current income, and more. By choosing to be positive, you can completely transform your life!

When you combine a positive mindset with positive habits, you become *unstoppable* – literally. You can heal your life, relieve stress, attract abundance, live peacefully, and yes, actually attain your happily ever after. It all starts with the *energy* you feed into your mind, what *beliefs* you create, and how you allow that energy to direct your daily *habits*.

This journal was *intentionally* created to help you rewire your mind for positivity, to empower you to focus on the positive, and to give you the tools to choose positivity, easily and regularly –

even during negatively charged circumstances. I want you to be charged by positivity every single day.

I know you want to be more positive, or you wouldn't be here, reading these words. Every morning, when you sit down to write in this journal, you are teaching yourself how to choose more positive thoughts. Every evening, as you sit down to answer the end-of-the-day prompts, you are reinforcing these new positive mental habits.

Being positive is a lifestyle that takes commitment and practice, especially if you didn't have positive role models or examples growing up. Optimism is not an impossible mindset to achieve, and it doesn't take long to form the right habits to be more positive.

Before we talk about the specifics of each journal entry and why each section is included, let's dive into some common misunderstandings around positivity.

WHAT POSITIVITY IS NOT . . .

Positive thinking is not ignoring negative emotions.

Living a positive lifestyle is not about magically waking up and feeling positive while ignoring or rejecting anything that triggers negative emotion. In fact, that's furthest from the truth. What triggers you is awakening you to what needs your attention.

Negativity reveals to you the "red flags" in your day-to-day and in your life. It's essential to watch for negative patterns and cycles. Once you are aware of them, then you can heal and release these patterns in order to evolve into the version of who you truly are. Embracing a positive lifestyle is always about transforming and/or releasing negativity, never ignoring it.

In fact, you never want to hide or deflect any of your emotions – this is why we have a morning feelings check-in and evening "Mental Health Check." Journaling is the perfect way to process, understand and shift your feelings, so you don't get stuck.

When tough circumstances hit us with negative emotions, they come to us and flow like waves in an ocean. They are not meant to move in and become part of our identity. They come to teach us. To help us grow. To heal and *awaken us* to something we aren't paying attention to. But, the truth is, the longer we ignore them, the longer they stay, the bigger they become, the more of our life they consume, and the harder they are to release or transform. This is why I have included daily prompts in this journal to help you acknowledge and release your emotions, so they never go ignored.

Positive living is not about being a perfect human.

Striving for a joyful life is key, but it's not realistic to expect perfection and "positive vibes only" all the time. You are a human being, so please don't beat yourself up when something unexpected happens. Be gentle and patient with yourself.

Positivity is an amazing tool to help us navigate life, but we are constantly learning and growing. We will never reach perfection and that's okay.

If we expect perfection from ourselves, it will actually have a counter effect on us and the belief systems we hold. When we live with positivity, we strive to do our best and improve our life, but we know that it's okay when we make mistakes or experience failure. That's when we can learn and grow the most. A positive outlook shows us that failure can transform into *feedback* to help us become a better version of ourselves.

Positivity is not toxic.

Positive thinking is not pretending that everything is okay, even when it's not. This way of thinking has coined the trendy term "toxic positivity." This is not something we encourage or embrace.

Life is constantly trying to balance itself. So it's vital to realize adversity happens; grief and suffering occur. Especially when you have a big, open heart and love someone or something deeply, pain is going to surface. It's a part of being alive.

There are many ways in which we can work toward healing the pain that arises within us so we can live more positive, enjoyable lives. Some of these positive habits are covered in this journal. Others include surrounding yourself with high-vibrational positive people who care, diving deep into self-care, reading transformative books, being gentle and loving with your self-talk, and doing things that make you feel good. These are positive habits that can help alleviate the pain, and prevent you from hitting rock bottom.

Emotions are our guides, and living a positive life is about learning to be flexible in the waves of change and adjusting our course as needed.

Positivity is not selfish.

When we talk about living a positive lifestyle in our community, we talk a lot about self-care and surrounding ourselves with positive people. Self-care is not selfish. In fact, it is the most selfless thing we can do, because without proper self-care, we cannot care for others properly. We must fill our cup and allow it to overflow. Feeling good and nurturing our mental health are two of our greatest responsibilities as humans.

Imagine someone you care about deeply who does not take care of her or himself physically or mentally. How much strain does their self-neglect place on your relationship with them?

"If you don't love yourself, nobody will. Not only that, you won't be good at loving anyone else. Loving starts with the self."

—WAYNE DYER

When we show up for ourselves and take care of ourselves physically, mentally, and spiritually, not only do we improve the length and quality of our lives, we also improve the depth and enjoyability of our relationships.

Researchers studying healthy self-esteem say that self-love helps to promote positive mental health and well-being.

Self-love is linked to a decrease in sadness, depression and loneliness, and an increase in well-being, both in relationships with ourselves and others. Having a healthy self-esteem also contributes to less feelings of anxiety and neuroticism.

All that to say, it's definitely not selfish for you to feel good and enjoy your life to its fullest.

WHAT POSITIVITY IS . . .

Positivity is about gratitude.

Gratitude is pivotal in living a genuinely happy life filled with positivity. I believe it's also the fuel for inner growth, abundance, expansion, and contentment. It is the key that unlocks the doors to achieve more. I know personally that this simple routine of giving thanks has been THE MOST profound one in my transformation – and it continues to be.

Even science agrees. According to Harvard Health, gratitude is a powerful emotion that attracts positivity and greater happiness.

When practiced consistently, positive emotions and experiences become second nature. Gratitude can improve health, lower stress levels, shield you from negative effects of any life circumstance, and help you build strong relationships.

You can experience gratitude in many different ways. Although it's never advised to dwell on your past, especially if it's filled with negativity, one way to make peace with it is to retrieve memories of the past and simply be thankful for them. Like every cloud has a silver lining, every negative situation has its own positives. To rewire your brain and to prevent the mind from creating emotion or thought hurdles from past negative situations, convert these negative emotions into positive ones by being thankful for the positive aspects of it.

Another way to practice gratitude and attract positivity is through the realization that nothing in your life is permanent. This will allow you to not take anything and anyone for granted.

Would you still be frustrated by your kids if you knew that this era in their lives will pass before you know it? That there will come a time when they are much older and much more independent.

Something quite powerful happens when we realize that our experiences are fleeting and that they will inevitably change into new realities.

When you live from a grateful heart, everything you "have to" do starts to shift into things you "get to" do.

It's impossible to create a positive life with a negative mind. The challenge with negativity is that sometimes it becomes a strong emotion that makes us forget everything good we have in our lives. This is why it's vital that you don't skip either of the morning and evening Gratitude Checks.

We've been doing these Gratitude Checks with our Power of Positivity community for over twelve years. The results and messages we continue to receive are astounding. People's lives begin to shift almost instantly as they begin to practice gratitude. When they make it a habit to regularly access and dwell in gratitude, the transformation they experience feels easy and miraculous.

The key secret to having more of what you want in your life is to be grateful for what you have right now. Stay mindful and happily present while excited about what is coming next. It's a careful balance, yes, but if you tune it right, you'll begin to unlock the transformative power of gratitude in your life.

Positive thinking fuels self-esteem.

Our self-esteem is built on two things: our self-image and our self-talk. Having a healthy relationship with ourselves, putting our own needs first, and loving ourselves creates an unshakable foundation from which we can build a fulfilling life bursting full of confidence and optimism.

Too little self-esteem can lead to higher levels of aggression and antisocial behavior. In order to feel positive, we must release negative self-talk and limiting belief systems – replacing them with positive affirmations and autosuggestions.

This is why becoming more positive often requires becoming aware of your mindset and emotions so that when a negative belief does arise you can identify it and try to understand what it is telling you, so you can transform it.

The same way that a caterpillar turns into a butterfly, there is a process. When we transform our limiting beliefs and boost our self-esteem, we can be all we were meant to be and radiate positivity. I will cover more about this in the section specifically about your daily affirmations.

Positivity is a tool for well-being.

Positivity rewires our bodies and brains on a cellular level for improved health. Studies show that our mental, physical, psychological, and even spiritual well-being improves significantly when we prioritize positive thoughts, actions, and emotions in our lives. This is why positivity is such an important and even vital part of our self-care routine.

Positivity is a mindset practice that affects every part of our being. This is why we have included a "Self-Care Check" in the morning to keep you conscious of the areas in your life that crave your attention. The "Wellness Check" in the evening also functions as a daily reminder and accountability for the mental habits that promote well-being.

Thoughts
Beliefs
Words
Actions
\+ Habits

= Life

Keep it positive!

Positive thoughts create positive habits.

Thoughts, words and actions guide us. Habits get us to our destination. What do your daily routines say about where you are going?

Take the habit of journaling for example. Studies show that the simple habit of putting pen to paper can help alleviate symptoms of depression, reduce anxiety, calm and clear your mind, manage stress, break down negative thought patterns, and help in injury recovery. People who journal daily tend to be more introspective, more connected to their emotions, more at peace, and more positive.

It may feel awkward when you begin to journal, unless you have done it before. That's okay. There is no right or wrong way to do it. I've made it easy for you with quick, time-efficient check-in's that will instantly boost your mood. In fact, as you begin to build this daily habit, you will notice an immediate shift within just the first few days.

As you train your mind to do these check-ins automatically, your life will begin to improve.

Over time, the pages in this book will become your *peaceful* respite to stop overthinking and begin fueling your mind with daily positivity. This journal has the power to uplift you, guide you, and change the direction of your whole day!

"Negative emotions have an important role to play in a happy life; they're big, flashing signs that something needs to change."

—GRETCHEN RUBIN

Positivity vs. Negativity

We can't really talk about positivity without acknowledging negativity. So many people get stuck in negative thought patterns that create negative beliefs that result in negative self-talk and negative action, which feed negative habits that perpetuate cycles of negativity in their lives. While it's far more effective to focus on positivity and building positive habits, we do need to know how to work with and through negativity that is persistent and loud. For this reason, I've decided to share a simple tool with you that will help you soften or dissolve the negativity that might be present in your life.

Use this tool as needed, but know that life becomes far more enjoyable and productive when we focus on what we're creating and fostering rather than what we're fighting or releasing. Whenever you can, focus on positivity. Use this tool when your negative thoughts are getting in your way of doing that.

HOW TO RELEASE NEGATIVITY

There is a specific process you can use to heal and release negativity when it arises. I call this the **RARE METHOD**: Recognize, Accept, Redefine, and Evolve (RARE).

The RARE Method is all about discovery, cleansing, and growth. With it, you can dissolve the negativity and free yourself of destructive life patterns. RARE, as the acronym suggests, is a rare and beautiful way of experiencing life with a *fresh perspective*, because there are greener pastures on the other side of negativity.

An old Chinese proverb says, "The gem cannot be polished without friction, nor a person perfected without trials."

While it is true that friction and contrast are necessary for our growth and evolution, living a life full of trials is not fulfilling our purpose. That's where the RARE Method can help us in healing and transforming.

Using the RARE Method, you can transform any negative situation by following these four simple steps:

1. Recognize the negativity,
2. Accept it,
3. Redefine the situation, and
4. Evolve into the best version of who you are.

True healing begins when we choose to accept the negativity. Although it's the most challenging part, acceptance of what is present helps us make peace with it so we can redefine and ultimately release the negativity, which will then allow us to improve and evolve.

1. Recognizing the Negativity

Everything we experience, all our thoughts and emotions, are recorded in our subconscious mind. It's literally our "sub" conscious, the thoughts *under* our conscious thought processes. Most of our life runs on autopilot, and comes from signals created here. All too often, we don't even realize that we are harboring negative beliefs about ourselves and others, because they have become so much a part of who we think we are.

Sometimes the unhealed parts become obvious when we are conscious of an emotional trigger, a destructive pattern, an addiction, or a repetitive cycle that keeps us stuck. Recognizing these negative patterns is the first step toward redefining and releasing them.

I've included feeling and mental health check-ins in this journal to help you become aware of how you are feeling, so you can more easily recognize the underlying emotions that are running your life and actions. After we recognize the root cause of our negativity or the triggers that cause us to respond negatively, we can move onto the next stages, thereby changing how we react to the negativity.

2. Accepting the Negativity

Once you've recognized the negativity and/or the triggers that are present in your life, you can take the next step and accept it.

Acceptance is not agreement. Acceptance does not mean that you agree with the thoughts that are present or that you believe they are true. Acceptance means that you acknowledge that these thoughts and these emotions are present within you without trying to fight or change them.

Feelings are not facts.
Thoughts are not facts.

Accepting them as the reality of this moment does not make them true forever in every moment.

Often, the very act of accepting what you feel will begin to soften that feeling. When you stop fighting or judging what is present, you give yourself permission to redefine, release, and replace it.

3. Redefining the Negativity

Redefining means "to define again or [define] differently." After recognizing and accepting the negativity, you can redefine how you feel about that particular negative emotion or event. Redefine requires you **to release your current feelings about that situation** and change the story – thereby, redefining it.

> How else can you look at this situation?
> Is there a different perspective?
> What other stories can you tell about it?

In order to redefine the negativity, we must be willing to challenge our existing interpretation of events. We have to be willing to see things differently and change our mind.

Redefining makes us realize that it's never an event that makes us suffer, but rather our interpretation of that event. If I get bullied in school, for example, I will feel very differently about the bullying if I interpret it as "I am weak and unlovable," or as "The bullying has nothing to do with me. It's a coping mechanism used by a kid who is working through his own insecurities, fears, and feelings of inadequacy." In one instance, my self-esteem and ability to love myself might be shattered. While in the second, I might realize it wasn't my fault and feel compassion for the very person who once hurt me. In either scenario, the event is in the past and the immediate pain is long gone, what remains are the stories I tell of the event.

One powerful way to redefine feelings is through positive affirmations or autosuggestions. Positive affirmations can help dissolve false or negative belief systems by reprogramming the mind. This is why I've included daily prompts for you to practice your personal affirmations. I want you to begin flipping the script in areas of your life that aren't ideal.

I've also flipped the script on negative stories during meditation or deep thinking and self-talk. With a positive perspective, you can forgive people and difficult life circumstances. You can see things in a new way.

"Being negative only makes the journey more difficult. You may be given a cactus, but you don't have to sit on it ..."

—JOYCE MEYER

I love Tony Robbins' perspective, "Life is happening for you, not to you." When I fully embraced that statement, I was able to let go of so much baggage.

I started to see negative experiences as *gifts for growth* rather than *pain without purpose.*

4. Evolving from the Negativity

The most beautiful thing about being a human is that we can transform into positive beings filled with warmth, love and gratitude in our hearts. When you redefine negativity, you make space for positivity to shine through you. As a result, you evolve and become a peaceful and loving version of you, who focuses on the silver linings.

Every situation comes with its own set of consequences that can be interpreted in positive or negative ways. We evolve when we see the less-than-ideal outcomes as guides to help us grow. When we realize that life is always working out for us, we're able to see every adverse situation as an opportunity to evolve.

Change is necessary to release negativity for good.

Your minds wants to be the one in control. When you try to change something in your life, your mind knows that this change might disrupt. This is why whenever you decide to make a change, it creates thought hurdles as a way to stop you from taking action that is new or different. Bob Proctor calls this the Paradigm.

According to Bob Proctor, "Paradigms are a multitude of habits that guide every move you make. They affect the way you eat, the way you walk, even the way you talk. They govern your communication, your work habits, your successes and your failures."

This explains why some people get where they want to be in life with minimal effort and others struggle to take a simple step. The problem isn't you; the problem is your paradigms. In order to change the quality of our lives, we must shift our paradigms, alter or replace existing ones with new, positive ones.

Bob Proctor says, "There will be no permanent change in your life until the paradigm has been changed."

As you shift from a negative mindset to a positive one, know that this change might not be easy in the beginning, and be gentle with yourself. Allow yourself to shift gradually by engaging with this journal every day. Before you know it, being positive will become the easier of the two paths.

ADDITIONAL RESOURCES

The topic of negativity, wounds, triggers, false beliefs, etc. is a big one. This journal will help you work through many of these by continually refocusing your mind on positive mental habits. Still, you might find that you need additional support to release negativity, rewrite limiting beliefs, and heal old wounds.

Sometimes when the past is too heavy to handle on our own, it's time to seek help from professionals. I have tried and highly recommend any form of talk therapy, prayer, light therapy, sound healing, neurofeedback, tapping, auto suggestions, and guided meditation – just to name a few.

You can also dig deeper into transformative work on your own by reading books written by some of the world's most effective personal development experts.

Here are a few of my favorite books on personal development. Pick up the one that resonates with you, and dive in. Couple the reading of these books with your journaling practice to experience transformative results:

- Norman Vincent Peale, *The Power of Positive Thinking*
- Wayne Dyer, *10 Secrets for Success and Inner Peace*
- Florence Scovel Shinn, *The Magic Path of Intuition*
- Rhonda Byrne, *The Secret*
- Eckhart Tolle, *The Power of Now*
- Deepak Chopra, *The Seven Spiritual Laws of Success*
- Lewis Howes, *The School of Greatness*
- Vex King, *Good Vibes, Good Life*
- Louise Hay, *You Can Heal Your Life*
- Dr. Nicole LePera, *How to Do the Work*
- Dr. Bradley Nelson, *The Emotion Code*
- Dr. Joe Dispenza, *Evolve Your Brain* and *Breaking the Habit of Being Yourself*
- James Clear, *Atomic Habits*
- Napoleon Hill, *Think and Grow Rich*
- Don Miguel Ruiz, *The Four Agreements*
- Brené Brown, *The Gifts of Imperfection*
- Louise Hay, *Mirror Work*
- Stephen Covey, *The 7 Habits of Highly Effective People*

Once you address and release negativity, you create space within yourself and within your life. When you create space, you allow for newness to enter. This newness, in my opinion, is really just more access and knowing of who you truly are and what you are capable of. It's transforming pain into love. It's always been there, but there was clutter and mess in the way.

Evolving into who you really are is an ongoing process. As long as you draw breath, you are on this path of becoming more. Positivity is the path that leads us to our full potential. I am excited for you as you step more fully onto this path toward who you really are and what you're here to accomplish!

"Focus your energy on everything that feeds your purpose, deepens your peace, and fuels a positive mindset. Everything else is wasted energy. Let the negativity go!"

@LEWISHOWES

How To Use This Journal

Positive people have trained their mind to be positive. When you meet someone who glistens with optimism, this was no accident. Habits that they commit to daily have helped them choose to see the good repeatedly until positivity became a natural habit for them over time. Some of the most positive people I have met were not given an easy life. They create strength and happiness from dark places.

In this journal, we are going to create strength and happiness from wherever you are right now – that may be a dark place or a may be a place that isn't exactly where you'd like to be. Either way, we are in this together, are you ready to get unstuck? Yes!

PART 1 – MORNING INTENTIONS

Your morning routine is everything! It sets the tone for your day. It gives you the opportunity to have a fresh start, a new perspective. Numerous studies have found that the attitude you have in the morning is usually the one that will stick with you throughout the day.

In this journal, I've included many of the practices that positive people engage in on a daily basis. This is why the morning entries include inspiration, mental health check, gratitude, mindfulness, positive self-talk, affirmations, and self-care. Fall in love with starting your day with these positivity practices, and watch your life transform from one day to the next. Now, let's dive in!

Inspirational Quote

Every morning begins with a daily inspirational quote. Starting your morning with wisdom and motivation will set the tone for the rest of your journal entry and your day.

Positive quotes help reinforce positivity into your day and boost your mood. They help pick you up from where you are and place you where you want to be – sometimes not immediately, but every quote adds up. And, if just one in the morning is not enough, remember the PoP community has hundreds of thousands of free quote posters available to you on our website and on all of our social media channels. I know first-hand how powerful inspirational quotes are and that's why I've included one at the top of every morning entry.

Mental Health Check

The next section of the journal is a mood check-in. Here you take a few moments to be mindful about how you are feeling at the start of your entry. Emotional intelligence is a great indicator for success and happiness. Learning to recognize and accept how you feel is the key to letting go and moving to better feelings. This quick exercise helps you stop the habit of ignoring, numbing or stuffing your feelings down. Instead, you'll identify, label, accept, and move towards a better feeling.

May anything that is
bothering you be solved,
healed or released every day.

If you've never paid attention to your feelings, you might have a hard time with this check in. Take your time with it, and be gentle with yourself. Soon, you'll be a pro at identifying your emotions.

To start, take a few deep breaths, put your hand on your heart or chest and check in with yourself. Feel the sensations of your body. Some days will be easier than others to recognize your true feelings. When you've identified your exact mood, answer honestly by circling the emoji that closely resembles. If none, create your own in the space. Then, in the space provided, write down how you would like to feel if you could choose your emotions.

After you write down your response, strategize with yourself about how you might be able to get from what you are feeling right now to how you would like to feel. If this is something you'd like to journal about, there is ample space at the bottom of the entry and at the back of this journal.

Finally, if you ever have trouble identifying the exact emotion, that's okay, we highly recommend the "Mood Meter" app. Your emotions affect your actions and, sometimes, the outcome of your entire day. Set yourself up for a better-feeling day by tuning into this important, mindful practice.

Gratitude Check

Every day is a fresh start.
Wake up with a grateful heart.

Gratitude turns what we have into enough. It allows us to fully appreciate the present moment and be mindful of what is good in our lives. It is also one of THE MOST powerful aspects of positivity. I credit it to being the key element in transforming my life and so do millions of other people around the world. This is why I've included gratitude both in the morning and evening entries in this journal.

There's a plethora of research that shows how powerful gratitude is in the morning. When you start your day with a grateful heart you set yourself up for a day of opportunities. You say "Yes!" to abundance and turn yourself into a magnet for everything that you desire.

Feeling truly appreciative for the big and small blessings in our lives teaches our brain to focus more on the positive aspects as opposed to the negative ones. This shift in thinking helps minimize the impact that day-to-day external frustrations can have on our lives.

GRATITUDE CHECK

TODAY I AM GRATEFUL FOR . . .

1. ....

2. ....

3. ....

In this journal, we're asking you to write down three things you are grateful for in the morning and three things in the evening. Over time, this simple gratitude practice will create a domino effect. You'll start naturally feeling grateful throughout the day as you find reasons to acknowledge feeling thankful. It will become second nature.

"The struggle ends when gratitude begins."

—NEALE DONALD WALSCH

Gratitude is deceptively simple and surprisingly powerful. It is one of the easiest and most effective ways to drastically improve the quality of your life with minimal effort. So, don't skip it!

Daily Affirmations

The words we use shape our reality. They are the blueprint for our experiences. This is why affirmations are so powerful. We are always saying affirmations to ourselves without realizing it. The more frequently we affirm something to ourselves, the more ingrained it becomes in our subconscious mind. Most people will use affirmations that limit them, and they'll use these affirmations daily. They'll say things like:

- I'm not good at that.
- I've never been good with money.
- I can't ever lose weight.
- Learning something new is hard for me.
- My life is hard.
- I'm just not lucky.
- I never have nice things.
- I'm not talented enough.

This is just a small sampling of negative affirmations that people will use to hold themselves back from their potential. The list goes on!

Pay close attention to the sentences you speak out loud. Are you using limiting affirmations to create more of what you don't want in your life?

Affirmations, when used intentionally and positively, can help dissolve false belief systems by reprogramming your subconscious mind.

Follow these simple guidelines to create your own positive affirmations:

1. Make sure your affirmation expresses something you WANT to accomplish instead of something you want to avoid.

   Example: "I am financially abundant," rather than "I don't have debt."

2. State your affirmation in the present tense as though it has already happened and is a part of your current reality.

   Example: "I'm in a loving relationship with the love of my life," instead of "I'm going to date someone who doesn't cheat on me."

3. Be sure your affirmation makes you feel excited rather than doubtful or afraid.

   Example: If "I'm a multi-millionaire" makes you think, *Yeah, right!* Then go with, "I'm attracting more abundance into my life."

4. Build bridges for the things you don't yet believe by using "I'm in the process of," or "I'm learning to."

   Example: "I'm in the process of creating wealth in my life." "I'm learning to manifest my dream home."

Using the guidelines above, complete the following affirmation exercise. Create as many affirmations as you like (at least three), then pick the three that feel most immediate or resonate with you most. Once you have your top three affirmations, go to the first

DAILY AFFIRMATIONS

1. ....

2. ....

3. ....

Bonus: Read each affirmation 10x in the mirror & throughout the day for faster results.

page of the journal, and write them into the three slots provided under "Daily Affirmations." You will carry these affirmations forward with you until they serve their purpose and you feel you've fully embodied them. Then, you can return here and grab one or more affirmations to work on, or you can write new ones.

Affirmations help you feel better equipped in the areas you want to see change, improvement, and/or growth. When you write down these affirmations every day in the space provided, you strengthen these synapses in your brain. You make these affirmations a part of your daily reality.

For even better results, I recommend adding Louise Hay's method called "Mirror Work." This involves speaking your affirmations aloud to yourself, while looking into your own eyes. Recite each one at least ten times. If you find yourself short on time, say these affirmations aloud to yourself and be mindful the next time you have a chance to practice them in the mirror.

Remember, these statements have the power to take you anywhere you wish to go, so be generous with yourself. Speak into reality exactly what you want. Don't hold back. If what you want feels too far outside of your current reality, build a bridge to it by using Guideline #4.

Tap into who you truly are and your potential for greatness. Speak it into existence every day, and soon, it will become your reality.

Be gentle with yourself, affirmations are powerful and, sometimes, emotional. Keep moving along with the first three until you embody them. Then, come back to this chapter to grab new ones from the list you created or to create new ones.

Finally, have fun with this! Affirmations help us enter a state of flow in our physical reality so we can get to our destinations with less effort and more ease. Let them do their thing and enjoy the process.

Goal Setting

Studies show that people who write down their goals on paper are 42% more likely to achieve them than people who don't. That's why I've included a morning goal setting routine after your daily affirmations.

3 PRIORITY GOALS

1. ....
2. ....
3. ....

To-do lists can quickly become long and overwhelming. I love a good list, but sometimes they can actually get in our way of getting things done. This is why I find it extremely powerful to pick only three things to complete every single day.

Ask yourself: "What are the three things I can do today that will move me close to my goals?" or "What are three things that I absolutely need to get done today?"

One recommendation I have, and this is something that has changed my life significantly, is to make these to-do items small and bite-sized. Split large projects up into small action steps, and focus on completing only three of these small action steps every day. For example, if you wanted to redesign your office, you might break up the action into several small steps including: Go through this year's files, go through last year's files, donate old furniture, research a new "look" and make a mood board, research new furniture for the office, pick a new wall color, paint the walls, move everything out of the office and into the spare room, look for new drapes, look for a new rug, etc.

The idea is that every item will be something you can accomplish easily in just a few hours. Suddenly the daunting task of redesigning

"By recording your dreams and goals on paper, you set in motion the process of becoming the person you most want to be."

—MARK VICTOR HANSEN

your office becomes easy, because every step is specific and easy to accomplish.

Three small, bite-sized items per day are easy to manage. And the truth is, if you can get just three things done every single day, you'll get through your long to-do list far quicker than if you carry your to-do lists around with you for weeks, trying to find time for the large, daunting tasks that often weigh you down.

Self-Care Check

Self-care comes in many shapes. Sometimes, self-care is sleeping in a little longer. Sometimes, it's getting a massage. Sometimes, it's calling a friend or preparing a home-cooked meal for yourself. Whatever shape self-care takes for you, it's important that you complete at least one action every day that is purely in service to you.

As part of the Self-Care Check, I've included eight areas in which you can provide care and support for yourself. Check the ones that you want to focus on each day or as you complete them. It's your choice. Know that the examples I include below each area are only suggestions. I encourage you to fulfill the areas that resonate with you. Don't feel the need to overdo it — it's self-care after all.

YOU are the person who knows you and your needs best.

Self Care Check

- ☐ **PHYSICAL** Rest & recharge.
- ☐ **SOCIAL** Quality conversation.
- ☐ **SPIRITUAL** Good for the soul.
- ☐ **HOUSEHOLD** Cleaning or organizing.
- ☐ **PAMPERING** Treat yourself.
- ☐ **PERSONAL** Time on a hobby.
- ☐ **EMOTIONAL** Honor feelings.
- ☐ **MENTAL** Read or learn.

As such, YOU are the person who can best determine what you need on any given day to help you feel happier, more grounded, and more at peace.

It's an extremely powerful practice to do something for yourself each day. This habit will set you up for success every single day. It will help you feel loved and understood by the one person who knows you best and loves you most: YOU! As a result, you'll begin to feel loved, lovable, worthy, and whole in every area of your life and in every relationship.

My Thoughts & Notes

Finally, use this section to write out any additional notes, thoughts, or objectives. If you need additional space to write through your thoughts or emotions that may be coming up, you can find blank pages at the end of this journal.

Remember that writing by hand is a powerful practice. When we hand write something, the data goes straight to our brain's hippocampus, where it's analyzed. During the analyzing process, the brain decides what it wants to store as long-term memory and what it wants to discard. What you write has a higher chance of being stored as long-term memory than what you memorize. So, use these blank spaces to process what's coming up, release what is no longer serving you, and create new, positive neural pathways in your brain.

MY THOUGHTS & NOTES

30 Morning Positivity Habits

Morning habits and rituals are needed to sustain a good mood and positive vibes throughout the day. Studies show that 40% of people's morning day-to-day activities are beneficial to the rest of their day. Starting the day with a positive attitude through positive habits can work wonders on your productivity, activity levels, happiness, and success. Here are some morning habits that will help you wake up in a good mood, get positive vibes flowing, and have an amazing day!

- prayer
- gratitude
- journaling
- making your bed
- exercise
- meditation
- listening to a podcast
- declutter
- healthy breakfast
- fresh juice or smoothie
- going for a walk
- deep breathing
- gardening
- drinking water
- visualization
- sitting in silence
- forest bathing
- sun bathing
- writing
- cold shower
- sauna
- mastermind
- no tech
- "to be" list
- mindful tea or coffee
- meal planning
- hug your family
- send a good morning text
- read for 30 minutes
- dance to music

"I think it's very healthy to spend time alone. You need to know how to be alone and not defined by another person."

—OSCAR WILDE

PART 2 – EVENING REFLECTIONS

Like the morning, the evening is a magical time when we can rewrite our existing programming and develop lasting positive mental habits to guide our lives.

As our day starts to draw to a close, our brainwaves naturally begin to slow down. We start to drop from high Beta waves that are associated with trying to maneuver through a busy and often stress-filled day into the calmer Alpha and Theta waves. This is where our gateway into our subconscious mind opens up, and we gain access to the parts of our brain that are often hidden from our conscious mind.

This is why it's so damaging when we use our precious evenings frivolously by watching excessive television or consuming content that does not make us feel good. Watching the news right before bed, for example, is a particularly damaging habit that can get us locked into cycles of fear and stress. As a result, many people who have this habit of watching the news right before bed often feel helpless, fearful, stressed, and overwhelmed.

We can change our lives drastically simply by taking charge of our evenings. When you elevate your emotions right before bed, you not only set yourself up for a better tomorrow, but you also boost your immune system, you help your mind and your body to operate at a higher capacity, you cooperate with your own healing, and you set yourself up for expansion.

With this journal, I've made it easy for you to do this work efficiently and effectively. Every item on this list is carefully plucked from my own daily practices. I've chosen the exercises that have had the greatest positive impact on my life – practices that I know have the power to transform. So, participate in them willingly and enthusiastically, and allow your life as well as your mindset to transform through positivity.

Inspirational Quote

You can never get enough inspiration. The insights and wisdom shared by others give voice to our own internal discoveries and help solidify the lessons we're learning on a daily basis. This is why I've included a unique inspirational quote in the evening as well.

Gratitude Check

When you end your day with an attitude of gratitude, you trigger positive vibes and create long term positive memories in the subconscious, but that's only the beginning, there's much more to the equation.

Gratitude is often referred to as the emotion of creation. This is because gratitude turns us into a magnet for good things to come our way. The more gratitude we feel, the more blessings come our way.

> People who practice gratitude regularly often seem "lucky" to the outside world.

Things just seem to work out for them. The challenges that plague most of the world don't seem to affect them. This is not an accident. It is a byproduct of gratitude.

Gratitude also boosts our immune system. Studies have also found that grateful people get sick less and recover from illness faster. They live longer and look younger.

Living with a grateful heart is so powerful that you could change your entire life by this alone!! In fact, there are coaches and teachers whose entire curriculum revolves around helping you create a daily gratitude practice.

An evening gratitude practice can also help you fall asleep faster and sleep better at night. This alone is essential, since stress and a lack of sleep can lead to a wide range of health problems.

Wellness Check

This section is for you to celebrate some of the choices you've made that have contributed to your overall wellness. Did you work out today? Did you step outside into nature? Did you meditate? Did you make nutritious food choices? How many steps did you walk? Were you conscious about your caffeine intake? How many glasses of water did you drink?

I find that while most of us know that taking these wellness steps are good for our overall well-being, few of us actually prioritize them throughout the day. I believe that this is because we're not tracking them daily.

As a general rule, that which you track will expand, because whatever you're focusing your attention on will receive your energy. Most people will use this incredible phenomenon to create more suffering in their lives by focusing on and tracking all the things that go wrong for them throughout the day. At the end of the day, instead of focusing on what positive choices they made and what did work out for them, they'll focus their precious attention and energy on the opposite.

Don't be like most people. Be like the small minority who focus on the positive and therefore allow their blessings to expand.

As you complete this section, be sure to celebrate every box that you check and every glass that you circle. Don't get hung up on trying to check all of the boxes, though it would be wonderful if you did work up to doing that. Instead, give yourself a loving pat on the back for every decision that you made that day that brought wellness into your life.

MENTAL HEALTH CHECK

RIGHT NOW I FEEL . . . (YOU MAY CHOOSE MORE THAN ONE)

- ☐ HAPPY
- ☐ LOVING
- ☐ HOPEFUL
- ☐ CALM
- ☐ ANGRY
- ☐ OVERWHELMED
- ☐ PEACEFUL
- ☐ CREATIVE
- ☐ STRESSED
- ☐ ANNOYED
- ☐ POSITIVE
- ☐ ANXIOUS
- ☐ PROUD
- ☐ SAD
- ☐ TIRED
- ☐ SCARED
- ☐ JOYFUL
- ☐ ....

Mental Health Check

We've been talking a great deal about feelings. This is intentional, because most people are not in the habit of pausing and checking in with themselves.

So, be sure to take this opportunity at the end of the day to tune inward and ask yourself how you feel. You may select more than one emotion.

For added benefit, see if you can identify where in your body you experience this emotion. If you're feeling sad, how does this sadness manifest itself physically? Where do you feel this emotion? Then, if the emotion is one that does not feel good, see if you can take long steady belly breaths into this physical sensation until it releases a bit.

If you are struggling with emotions that are interfering with your ability to relax or enjoy your evening, focusing on the physical sensations rather than thoughts will help you release or at least soften these emotions, so you can find some relief from them.

Positivity Prompt

Positivity is a habit. It is an attitude - a way of life. As you have already seen in these pages, there are many different things we can do to live more positive lives. Every prompt I've included in this journal helps you become a more positive person.

"One day,
you will realize that
it had to happen, in that
way, to give you the
lessons you needed to
grow. What doesn't break
you forever only
makes you better."

@VEXKING

I do, however, want to share with you more tools, more ideas, and more ways that have helped me foster positivity within myself. This is why I have included a **Positivity Prompt** in the midst of your evening reflections.

These prompts change daily. They're designed to help you show up in more positive ways within your life. You might find that you already do some of these already, in which case, celebrate yourself as you answer the day's question. If you encounter a prompt that feels outside of what's natural for you, however, be gentle with yourself. For added benefit, see if you can do the suggested prompt the next day, and see how you feel as a result.

Wins for the Day

Most dinner conversations are filled with what went wrong, who made what mistake, and what drama unfolded that day. I would love for you to flip the script and make it a habit of asking this simple question: **"What went right today?"**

WINS FOR THE DAY

TODAY I ACCOMPLISHED . . .

....

....

....

....

You can ask this question when you're sitting at dinner with your family, when you're relaxing on the sofa with your partner at the end of a full day, or even at the end of a team meeting at work.

No matter when you ask this question, you'll at first encounter puzzled looks. Most people are not used to asking and answering this question. But this is precisely the **right question** to ask if you want to set yourself, your family, and your team up for more success.

I've included this "Wins" section, so you can build the muscle of acknowledging when things go right. Write down three things each day that went right and made you feel like a winner. Then, for added impact in your life, see if you can tap into the emotion of being a winner.

When we focus on our wins,
we give ourselves permission to
win more often.

My Thoughts & Notes

Use this area to clear out anything that's still weighing you down or staying on your mind.

You can more easily work through
it when you write through it.

If something is present within your thoughts, write it out and leave it on the page. If you need any additional space, be sure to flip to the end of this journal and fill in those empty pages.

Make a decision to talk about why
you're blessed, not stressed. You
give life to what you focus on.

30 Evening Positivity Habits

Evening habits and rituals are needed to relax and unwind, destress and get ready for a great night's sleep. Ending the day intentionally with a positive attitude through positive habits can set you up for success the next day. Here are some evening habits that will help you end the day the right way.

- prayer
- gratitude list
- journaling
- dim the lights
- meditation
- listening to a podcast
- homemade dinner
- go for a walk
- deep breathing
- drinking water
- take your vitamins/meds
- sitting in silence
- forest bathing
- quiet time
- writing
- sauna
- mastermind
- no tech
- let go of negativity
- epsom salt bath
- herbal tea
- intentional shower
- do something you love
- organize or tidy up
- skincare routine
- exercise to destress
- read for 30 minutes
- call/text family or a friend
- prepare for the next day
- pj's and downtime

"Please quit overthinking everything. Stop obsessing over your failures. Stop doubting yourself and seeing greatness in everyone else but you. You are better than that. You deserve more. Start showing up differently."

@LEWISHOWES

EXAMPLE ENTRY

MORNING INTENTIONS

DATE: 11 / 01 / 21

Everyday is a day to shine. Shine on! @powerofpositivity

I FEEL . . . I WANT TO FEEL creative & happy

GRATITUDE CHECK

TODAY I AM GRATEFUL FOR . . .

1. Waking up healthy.
2. My beautiful family.
3. A job that supports me.

TIME FOR DEEP BELLY BREATHS. GET COMFORTABLE. BREATHE IN SLOWLY AND COUNT TO 5. FILL YOUR BELLY LIKE A BALLOON. HOLD. BREATHE OUT SLOWLY THROUGH YOUR MOUTH. REPEAT OFTEN.

DAILY AFFIRMATIONS

1. I am healthy & strong. My body supports me.
2. I am choosing to feel happy today.
3. I am enough exactly as I am right now.

Bonus: Read each affirmation 10x in the mirror & throughout the day for faster results.

3 PRIORITY GOALS

1. Finish house chores.
2. Call my dad.
3. Meal plan for week.

Self Care Check

- [ ] **PHYSICAL** Rest & recharge.
- [ ] **SOCIAL** Quality conversation.
- [x] **SPIRITUAL** Good for the soul.
- [x] **HOUSEHOLD** Cleaning or organizing.
- [ ] **PAMPERING** Treat yourself.
- [ ] **PERSONAL** Time on a hobby.
- [x] **EMOTIONAL** Honor feelings.
- [ ] **MENTAL** Read or learn.

MY THOUGHTS & NOTES

I felt so much more relaxed after I took deep belly breaths.
I repeated often and it made all the difference.

EXAMPLE ENTRY

EVENING REFLECTIONS

DATE: 11 / 01 / 21

Always end the night with a positive thought. The day may have not been perfect, but keep your focus on what you want to expand. @powerofpositivity

GRATITUDE CHECK

TONIGHT I AM GRATEFUL FOR . . .

1. Delicious dinner.
2. Time with family.
3. Body that supports me.

Wellness Check

- [x] WORKOUT
- [x] NATURE
- [ ] MEDITATION
- CAFFEINE: 2 cups
- [ ] NUTRITION
- STEPS: 10,450

WATER INTAKE:

MENTAL HEALTH CHECK

RIGHT NOW I FEEL . . . (YOU MAY CHOOSE MORE THAN ONE)

- [ ] HAPPY
- [ ] LOVING
- [x] HOPEFUL
- [ ] CALM
- [ ] ANGRY
- [ ] OVERWHELMED
- [x] PEACEFUL
- [ ] CREATIVE
- [ ] STRESSED
- [ ] ANNOYED
- [ ] POSITIVE
- [ ] ANXIOUS
- [ ] PROUD
- [ ] SAD
- [x] TIRED
- [ ] SCARED
- [ ] JOYFUL
- [x] grateful

THE BIGGEST ACCOMPLISHMENT IN MY LIFE IS . . .

Having my children and living everyday with purpose and passion.

WINS FOR THE DAY

TODAY I ACCOMPLISHED . . .

My to do list of house chores.
I had a great call with dad.
Completed my meal planning + great workout.

MY THOUGHTS & NOTES

I love journaling more than I thought I would. It adds consistency to my day. I love checking in and accountability is helpful. I feel peaceful.

MORNING INTENTIONS

DATE: .... / .... / ....

Everyday is a day to shine. Shine on! @powerofpositivity

I FEEL . . . I WANT TO FEEL ....

GRATITUDE CHECK

TODAY I AM GRATEFUL FOR . . .

1. ....
2. ....
3. ....

TIME FOR DEEP BELLY BREATHS. GET COMFORTABLE. BREATHE IN SLOWLY AND COUNT TO 5. FILL YOUR BELLY LIKE A BALLOON. HOLD. BREATHE OUT SLOWLY THROUGH YOUR MOUTH. REPEAT OFTEN.

DAILY AFFIRMATIONS

1. ....
2. ....
3. ....

Bonus: Read each affirmation 10x in the mirror & throughout the day for faster results.

3 PRIORITY GOALS

1. ....
2. ....
3. ....

Self Care Check

- ☐ **PHYSICAL** Rest & recharge.
- ☐ **SOCIAL** Quality conversation.
- ☐ **SPIRITUAL** Good for the soul.
- ☐ **HOUSEHOLD** Cleaning or organizing.
- ☐ **PAMPERING** Treat yourself.
- ☐ **PERSONAL** Time on a hobby.
- ☐ **EMOTIONAL** Honor feelings.
- ☐ **MENTAL** Read or learn.

MY THOUGHTS & NOTES

EVENING REFLECTIONS

DATE: .... /........ /........

Always end the night with a positive thought. The day may have not been perfect, but keep your focus on what you want to expand. @powerofpositivity

GRATITUDE CHECK

TONIGHT I AM GRATEFUL FOR . . .

1. ....

2. ....

3. ....

Wellness Check

- ☐ **WORKOUT**
- ☐ **NATURE**
- ☐ **MEDITATION**
- **CAFFEINE:** ....
- ☐ **NUTRITION**
- **STEPS:** ....

WATER INTAKE:

MENTAL HEALTH CHECK

RIGHT NOW I FEEL . . . (YOU MAY CHOOSE MORE THAN ONE)

☐ HAPPY	☐ PEACEFUL	☐ PROUD
☐ LOVING	☐ CREATIVE	☐ SAD
☐ HOPEFUL	☐ STRESSED	☐ TIRED
☐ CALM	☐ ANNOYED	☐ SCARED
☐ ANGRY	☐ POSITIVE	☐ JOYFUL
☐ OVERWHELMED	☐ ANXIOUS	☐ ....

THE BIGGEST ACCOMPLISHMENT IN MY LIFE IS . . .

....

....

....

WINS FOR THE DAY

TODAY I ACCOMPLISHED . . .

....

....

....

....

MY THOUGHTS & NOTES

....

....

....

....

....

MORNING INTENTIONS

DATE: .... /........ /........

Sometimes it feels so good to just sit by yourself, relax and not talk to anyone. —Kristen Butler @positivekristen

I FEEL . . . I WANT TO FEEL ....

GRATITUDE CHECK

TODAY I AM GRATEFUL FOR . . .

1. ....
2. ....
3. ....

THINK BEFORE YOU SPEAK. STAY CONSCIOUS OF THE WORDS YOU SAY TODAY. COMPLIMENT YOURSELF AND OTHERS, BE THOUGHTFUL, GIVE HUGS, LAUGH, AND SPREAD POSITIVITY.

DAILY AFFIRMATIONS

1. ....
2. ....
3. ....

Bonus: Read each affirmation 10x in the mirror & throughout the day for faster results.

3 PRIORITY GOALS

1. ....
2. ....
3. ....

Self Care Check

- ☐ **PHYSICAL** Rest & recharge.
- ☐ **SOCIAL** Quality conversation.
- ☐ **SPIRITUAL** Good for the soul.
- ☐ **HOUSEHOLD** Cleaning or organizing.
- ☐ **PAMPERING** Treat yourself.
- ☐ **PERSONAL** Time on a hobby.
- ☐ **EMOTIONAL** Honor feelings.
- ☐ **MENTAL** Read or learn.

MY THOUGHTS & NOTES

EVENING REFLECTIONS

DATE: .... / .... / ....

What you think you become. What you feel you attract. What you imagine you create. —Buddha

GRATITUDE CHECK

TONIGHT I AM GRATEFUL FOR . . .

1. ....

2. ....

3. ....

Wellness Check

☐ **WORKOUT** ☐ **NATURE**

☐ **MEDITATION** **CAFFEINE:** ....

☐ **NUTRITION** **STEPS:** ....

WATER INTAKE:

MENTAL HEALTH CHECK

RIGHT NOW I FEEL . . . (YOU MAY CHOOSE MORE THAN ONE)

☐ HAPPY	☐ PEACEFUL	☐ PROUD
☐ LOVING	☐ CREATIVE	☐ SAD
☐ HOPEFUL	☐ STRESSED	☐ TIRED
☐ CALM	☐ ANNOYED	☐ SCARED
☐ ANGRY	☐ POSITIVE	☐ JOYFUL
☐ OVERWHELMED	☐ ANXIOUS	☐ ....

IS THERE ANYTHING I NEED TO LET GO OF FROM TODAY TO SLEEP PEACEFULLY TONIGHT?

....

....

....

WINS FOR THE DAY

TODAY I ACCOMPLISHED . . .

....

....

....

....

MY THOUGHTS & NOTES

....

....

....

....

....

MORNING INTENTIONS

DATE: .... /......... /.........

I act as if I already have what I want - it's an excellent way to attract happiness in my life. —Louise Hay

---

I FEEL . . . I WANT TO FEEL ....

GRATITUDE CHECK

TODAY I AM GRATEFUL FOR . . .

1. ....
2. ....
3. ....

TAKE 30 SECONDS TO IMAGINE EXACTLY HOW YOU WANT TO SEE YOURSELF IN 5 YEARS. FEEL THAT FEELING. WRITE IT DOWN. NOW KEEP IT WITH YOU TODAY.

DAILY AFFIRMATIONS

1. ....
2. ....
3. ....

Bonus: Read each affirmation 10x in the mirror & throughout the day for faster results.

3 PRIORITY GOALS

1. ....
2. ....
3. ....

Self Care Check

- ☐ **PHYSICAL** Rest & recharge.
- ☐ **SOCIAL** Quality conversation.
- ☐ **SPIRITUAL** Good for the soul.
- ☐ **HOUSEHOLD** Cleaning or organizing.
- ☐ **PAMPERING** Treat yourself.
- ☐ **PERSONAL** Time on a hobby.
- ☐ **EMOTIONAL** Honor feelings.
- ☐ **MENTAL** Read or learn.

MY THOUGHTS & NOTES

....

....

....

....

....

EVENING REFLECTIONS

DATE: .... /........ /........

The best way to cheer yourself up is to try to cheer someone else up.
—Mark Twain

GRATITUDE CHECK

TONIGHT I AM GRATEFUL FOR . . .

1. ....

2. ....

3. ....

Wellness Check

- ☐ **WORKOUT**
- ☐ **NATURE**
- ☐ **MEDITATION**
- **CAFFEINE:** ....
- ☐ **NUTRITION**
- **STEPS:** ....

WATER INTAKE:

MENTAL HEALTH CHECK

RIGHT NOW I FEEL . . . (YOU MAY CHOOSE MORE THAN ONE)

☐ HAPPY	☐ PEACEFUL	☐ PROUD
☐ LOVING	☐ CREATIVE	☐ SAD
☐ HOPEFUL	☐ STRESSED	☐ TIRED
☐ CALM	☐ ANNOYED	☐ SCARED
☐ ANGRY	☐ POSITIVE	☐ JOYFUL
☐ OVERWHELMED	☐ ANXIOUS	☐ ....

THREE THINGS THAT ALWAYS PUT ME IN A GOOD MOOD . . .

WINS FOR THE DAY

TODAY I ACCOMPLISHED . . .

MY THOUGHTS & NOTES

MORNING INTENTIONS

DATE: .... /........ /........

A journey of a thousand miles begins with a single step.
—Chinese Proverb

I FEEL . . . I WANT TO FEEL ....

GRATITUDE CHECK

TODAY I AM GRATEFUL FOR . . .

1. ....
2. ....
3. ....

IF YOU COULD GIVE YOURSELF ADVICE 10 YEARS AGO, WHAT WOULD IT BE? THINK ABOUT IT AND THEN FORGIVE YOURSELF FOR NOT KNOWING BETTER.

DAILY AFFIRMATIONS

1. ....
2. ....
3. ....

Bonus: Read each affirmation 10x in the mirror & throughout the day for faster results.

3 PRIORITY GOALS

1. ....
2. ....
3. ....

Self Care Check

- ☐ **PHYSICAL** Rest & recharge.
- ☐ **SOCIAL** Quality conversation.
- ☐ **SPIRITUAL** Good for the soul.
- ☐ **HOUSEHOLD** Cleaning or organizing.
- ☐ **PAMPERING** Treat yourself.
- ☐ **PERSONAL** Time on a hobby.
- ☐ **EMOTIONAL** Honor feelings.
- ☐ **MENTAL** Read or learn.

MY THOUGHTS & NOTES

....

....

....

....

....

EVENING REFLECTIONS

DATE: .... /........ /........

I do not fix my problems. I fix my thinking. Then the problems fix themselves. —Louise Hay

GRATITUDE CHECK

TONIGHT I AM GRATEFUL FOR . . .

1. ....

2. ....

3. ....

Wellness Check

☐ **WORKOUT** ☐ **NATURE**

☐ **MEDITATION** **CAFFEINE:** ....

☐ **NUTRITION** **STEPS:** ....

WATER INTAKE:

MENTAL HEALTH CHECK

RIGHT NOW I FEEL . . . (YOU MAY CHOOSE MORE THAN ONE)

☐ HAPPY	☐ PEACEFUL	☐ PROUD
☐ LOVING	☐ CREATIVE	☐ SAD
☐ HOPEFUL	☐ STRESSED	☐ TIRED
☐ CALM	☐ ANNOYED	☐ SCARED
☐ ANGRY	☐ POSITIVE	☐ JOYFUL
☐ OVERWHELMED	☐ ANXIOUS	☐ ....

HOW CAN I PAMPER MYSELF IN THE NEXT 24 HOURS?

....

....

....

WINS FOR THE DAY

TODAY I ACCOMPLISHED . . .

....

....

....

....

MY THOUGHTS & NOTES

....

....

....

....

....

MORNING INTENTIONS

DATE: .... /........ /........

When something I can't control happens, I ask myself; Where is this hidden gift? Where is the positive in this? —Sara Blakely @sarablakely

---

I FEEL . . . I WANT TO FEEL ....

GRATITUDE CHECK

TODAY I AM GRATEFUL FOR . . .

1. ....
2. ....
3. ....

TAKE TIME TO THINK ABOUT WHO AND WHAT MAKES YOU FEEL ALIVE. CAN YOU CONNECT WITH THAT PERSON TODAY? CAN YOU DO ONE OF THOSE ACTIVITIES THIS WEEK?

DAILY AFFIRMATIONS

1. ....
2. ....
3. ....

Bonus: Read each affirmation 10x in the mirror & throughout the day for faster results.

3 PRIORITY GOALS

1. ....
2. ....
3. ....

Self Care Check

- ☐ **PHYSICAL** Rest & recharge.
- ☐ **SOCIAL** Quality conversation.
- ☐ **SPIRITUAL** Good for the soul.
- ☐ **HOUSEHOLD** Cleaning or organizing.
- ☐ **PAMPERING** Treat yourself.
- ☐ **PERSONAL** Time on a hobby.
- ☐ **EMOTIONAL** Honor feelings.
- ☐ **MENTAL** Read or learn.

MY THOUGHTS & NOTES

EVENING REFLECTIONS

DATE: .... /........ /........

The energy you give out is what you give back. Think positive. Enjoy life. Send out good vibes. @powerofpositivity

---

GRATITUDE CHECK

TONIGHT I AM GRATEFUL FOR . . .

1. ....

2. ....

3. ....

Wellness Check

- ☐ **WORKOUT**
- ☐ **NATURE**
- ☐ **MEDITATION**
- **CAFFEINE:** ....
- ☐ **NUTRITION**
- **STEPS:** ....

WATER INTAKE:

MENTAL HEALTH CHECK

RIGHT NOW I FEEL . . . (YOU MAY CHOOSE MORE THAN ONE)

☐ HAPPY	☐ PEACEFUL	☐ PROUD
☐ LOVING	☐ CREATIVE	☐ SAD
☐ HOPEFUL	☐ STRESSED	☐ TIRED
☐ CALM	☐ ANNOYED	☐ SCARED
☐ ANGRY	☐ POSITIVE	☐ JOYFUL
☐ OVERWHELMED	☐ ANXIOUS	☐ ....

DO YOU APPRECIATE YOUR BODY? LIST GOOD THINGS IT DOES FOR YOU . . .

....

....

....

WINS FOR THE DAY

TODAY I ACCOMPLISHED . . .

....

....

....

....

MY THOUGHTS & NOTES

....

....

....

....

....

MORNING INTENTIONS

DATE: .... /........ /........

Set your mind up for success. Be the kind of person who refuses to give up. —Joyce Meyer @joycemeyer

---

I FEEL . . . I WANT TO FEEL ....

GRATITUDE CHECK

TODAY I AM GRATEFUL FOR . . .

1. ....
2. ....
3. ....

HOW MOTIVATED HAVE YOU BEEN FEELING LATELY? CHECK IN AND DECIDE IF IT'S TIME TO CRANK UP THE DIAL TO ACHIEVE YOUR GOALS.

DAILY AFFIRMATIONS

1. ....
2. ....
3. ....

Bonus: Read each affirmation 10x in the mirror & throughout the day for faster results.

3 PRIORITY GOALS

1. ....
2. ....
3. ....

Self Care Check

- ☐ **PHYSICAL** Rest & recharge.
- ☐ **SOCIAL** Quality conversation.
- ☐ **SPIRITUAL** Good for the soul.
- ☐ **HOUSEHOLD** Cleaning or organizing.
- ☐ **PAMPERING** Treat yourself.
- ☐ **PERSONAL** Time on a hobby.
- ☐ **EMOTIONAL** Honor feelings.
- ☐ **MENTAL** Read or learn.

MY THOUGHTS & NOTES

....

....

....

....

....

EVENING REFLECTIONS

DATE: .... /........ /........

When you focus on the positive, you feel better and you attract better. New doors open and bring the opportunities you seek. @powerofpositivity

GRATITUDE CHECK

TONIGHT I AM GRATEFUL FOR . . .

1. ....

2. ....

3. ....

Wellness Check

- ☐ **WORKOUT**
- ☐ **NATURE**
- ☐ **MEDITATION**
- **CAFFEINE:** ....
- ☐ **NUTRITION**
- **STEPS:** ....

WATER INTAKE:

MENTAL HEALTH CHECK

RIGHT NOW I FEEL . . . (YOU MAY CHOOSE MORE THAN ONE)

☐ HAPPY	☐ PEACEFUL	☐ PROUD
☐ LOVING	☐ CREATIVE	☐ SAD
☐ HOPEFUL	☐ STRESSED	☐ TIRED
☐ CALM	☐ ANNOYED	☐ SCARED
☐ ANGRY	☐ POSITIVE	☐ JOYFUL
☐ OVERWHELMED	☐ ANXIOUS	☐ ....

WRITE ABOUT A TIME WHEN YOU FELT COURAGEOUS . . .

....

....

....

WINS FOR THE DAY

TODAY I ACCOMPLISHED . . .

....

....

....

....

MY THOUGHTS & NOTES

....

....

....

....

....

MORNING INTENTIONS

DATE: .... /........ /........

A strong soul shines after every storm. —Kristen Butler
@positivekristen

I FEEL . . . I WANT TO FEEL ....

GRATITUDE CHECK

TODAY I AM GRATEFUL FOR . . .

1. ....
2. ....
3. ....

LAUGHTER IS THE BEST MEDICINE. DO ONE THING TODAY THAT MAKES YOU LAUGH UNTIL YOUR BELLY HURTS.

DAILY AFFIRMATIONS

1. ....
2. ....
3. ....

Bonus: Read each affirmation 10x in the mirror & throughout the day for faster results.

3 PRIORITY GOALS

1. ....
2. ....
3. ....

Self Care Check

- ☐ **PHYSICAL** Rest & recharge.
- ☐ **SOCIAL** Quality conversation.
- ☐ **SPIRITUAL** Good for the soul.
- ☐ **HOUSEHOLD** Cleaning or organizing.
- ☐ **PAMPERING** Treat yourself.
- ☐ **PERSONAL** Time on a hobby.
- ☐ **EMOTIONAL** Honor feelings.
- ☐ **MENTAL** Read or learn.

MY THOUGHTS & NOTES

....

....

....

....

....

EVENING REFLECTIONS

DATE: .... /........... /...........

Never give up on something that still makes you happy, even if it's tough. @powerofpositivity

GRATITUDE CHECK

TONIGHT I AM GRATEFUL FOR . . .

1. ....

2. ....

3. ....

Wellness Check

☐ **WORKOUT** ☐ **NATURE**

☐ **MEDITATION** **CAFFEINE:** ....

☐ **NUTRITION** **STEPS:** ....

WATER INTAKE:

MENTAL HEALTH CHECK

RIGHT NOW I FEEL . . . (YOU MAY CHOOSE MORE THAN ONE)

☐ HAPPY	☐ PEACEFUL	☐ PROUD
☐ LOVING	☐ CREATIVE	☐ SAD
☐ HOPEFUL	☐ STRESSED	☐ TIRED
☐ CALM	☐ ANNOYED	☐ SCARED
☐ ANGRY	☐ POSITIVE	☐ JOYFUL
☐ OVERWHELMED	☐ ANXIOUS	☐ ....

WRITE A HAPPY STORY IN ONLY 4 WORDS . . .

....

....

....

WINS FOR THE DAY

TODAY I ACCOMPLISHED . . .

....

....

....

....

MY THOUGHTS & NOTES

....

....

....

....

....

MORNING INTENTIONS

DATE: .... /........ /........

Good things are going to happen. Have faith and stay positive.
@powerofpositivity

I FEEL . . . I WANT TO FEEL ....

GRATITUDE CHECK

TODAY I AM GRATEFUL FOR . . .

1. ....
2. ....
3. ....

SOMETIMES NATURE IS ALL YOU NEED. DON'T FORGET TO ENJOY SOME LEVEL OF NATURE TODAY. THINK ABOUT YOUR FAVORITE LOCAL PLACE TO GO. NOW MAKE PLANS TO FIT IT IN.

DAILY AFFIRMATIONS

1. ....
2. ....
3. ....

Bonus: Read each affirmation 10x in the mirror & throughout the day for faster results.

3 PRIORITY GOALS

1. ....
2. ....
3. ....

Self Care Check

- ☐ **PHYSICAL** Rest & recharge.
- ☐ **SOCIAL** Quality conversation.
- ☐ **SPIRITUAL** Good for the soul.
- ☐ **HOUSEHOLD** Cleaning or organizing.
- ☐ **PAMPERING** Treat yourself.
- ☐ **PERSONAL** Time on a hobby.
- ☐ **EMOTIONAL** Honor feelings.
- ☐ **MENTAL** Read or learn.

MY THOUGHTS & NOTES

....

....

....

....

....

EVENING REFLECTIONS

DATE: .... /........ /........

Never give up on something that still makes you happy, even if it's tough. @powerofpositivity

GRATITUDE CHECK

TONIGHT I AM GRATEFUL FOR . . .

1. ....

2. ....

3. ....

Wellness Check

☐ **WORKOUT** ☐ **NATURE**

☐ **MEDITATION** **CAFFEINE:** ....

☐ **NUTRITION** **STEPS:** ....

WATER INTAKE:

MENTAL HEALTH CHECK

RIGHT NOW I FEEL . . . (YOU MAY CHOOSE MORE THAN ONE)

☐ HAPPY	☐ PEACEFUL	☐ PROUD
☐ LOVING	☐ CREATIVE	☐ SAD
☐ HOPEFUL	☐ STRESSED	☐ TIRED
☐ CALM	☐ ANNOYED	☐ SCARED
☐ ANGRY	☐ POSITIVE	☐ JOYFUL
☐ OVERWHELMED	☐ ANXIOUS	☐ ....

HOW CAN I HELP SOMEONE ELSE TOMORROW?

....

....

....

WINS FOR THE DAY

TODAY I ACCOMPLISHED . . .

....

....

....

....

MY THOUGHTS & NOTES

....

....

....

....

....

MORNING INTENTIONS

DATE: .... /........ /........

Every single thought is creating your future. Let that sink in.
@powerofpositivity

I FEEL . . . I WANT TO FEEL ....

GRATITUDE CHECK

TODAY I AM GRATEFUL FOR . . .

1. ....
2. ....
3. ....

DO YOU FEEL FINANCIALLY ABUNDANT? IF YOU ANSWERED A STRONG NO, IT MAY BE HELPFUL TO MAKE ONE OF YOUR AFFIRMATIONS REGARDING MONEY.

DAILY AFFIRMATIONS

1. ....
2. ....
3. ....

Bonus: Read each affirmation 10x in the mirror & throughout the day for faster results.

3 PRIORITY GOALS

1. ....
2. ....
3. ....

Self Care Check

☐ **PHYSICAL** Rest & recharge.

☐ **SOCIAL** Quality conversation.

☐ **SPIRITUAL** Good for the soul.

☐ **HOUSEHOLD** Cleaning or organizing.

☐ **PAMPERING** Treat yourself.

☐ **PERSONAL** Time on a hobby.

☐ **EMOTIONAL** Honor feelings.

☐ **MENTAL** Read or learn.

MY THOUGHTS & NOTES

....

....

....

....

....

EVENING REFLECTIONS

DATE: .... /......... /.........

My day wasn't perfect, but I'm thankful for everything I have. Even the challenges support my growth. @powerofpositivity

---

GRATITUDE CHECK

TONIGHT I AM GRATEFUL FOR . . .

1. ....

2. ....

3. ....

Wellness Check

☐ WORKOUT ☐ NATURE

☐ MEDITATION CAFFEINE: ....

☐ NUTRITION STEPS: ....

WATER INTAKE:

MENTAL HEALTH CHECK

RIGHT NOW I FEEL . . . (YOU MAY CHOOSE MORE THAN ONE)

☐ HAPPY	☐ PEACEFUL	☐ PROUD
☐ LOVING	☐ CREATIVE	☐ SAD
☐ HOPEFUL	☐ STRESSED	☐ TIRED
☐ CALM	☐ ANNOYED	☐ SCARED
☐ ANGRY	☐ POSITIVE	☐ JOYFUL
☐ OVERWHELMED	☐ ANXIOUS	☐ ....

HOW CAN I BRING MORE JOY INTO MY LIFE?

....

....

....

WINS FOR THE DAY

TODAY I ACCOMPLISHED . . .

....

....

....

....

MY THOUGHTS & NOTES

....

....

....

....

....

MORNING INTENTIONS

DATE: .... /........ /........

The journey of a thousand miles begins with one step. —Lao Tzu

I FEEL . . . I WANT TO FEEL ....

GRATITUDE CHECK

TODAY I AM GRATEFUL FOR . . .

1. ....
2. ....
3. ....

BE MINDFUL TODAY. WHEN YOU FEEL OFF BALANCE, DO SOMETHING IMMEDIATELY THAT WILL CENTER YOU. BE A TREE. STAND TALL AND STRONG.

DAILY AFFIRMATIONS

1. ....
2. ....
3. ....

Bonus: Read each affirmation 10x in the mirror & throughout the day for faster results.

3 PRIORITY GOALS

1. ....
2. ....
3. ....

Self Care Check

- ☐ **PHYSICAL** Rest & recharge.
- ☐ **SOCIAL** Quality conversation.
- ☐ **SPIRITUAL** Good for the soul.
- ☐ **HOUSEHOLD** Cleaning or organizing.
- ☐ **PAMPERING** Treat yourself.
- ☐ **PERSONAL** Time on a hobby.
- ☐ **EMOTIONAL** Honor feelings.
- ☐ **MENTAL** Read or learn.

MY THOUGHTS & NOTES

....

EVENING REFLECTIONS

DATE: .... /........ /........

No matter what happens today, never stop believing that you will make it through. Even if it isn't today, tomorrow is another chance.

GRATITUDE CHECK

TONIGHT I AM GRATEFUL FOR . . .

1. ....

2. ....

3. ....

Wellness Check

☐ **WORKOUT** ☐ **NATURE**

☐ **MEDITATION** **CAFFEINE:** ....

☐ **NUTRITION** **STEPS:** ....

WATER INTAKE:

MENTAL HEALTH CHECK

RIGHT NOW I FEEL . . . (YOU MAY CHOOSE MORE THAN ONE)

☐ HAPPY	☐ PEACEFUL	☐ PROUD
☐ LOVING	☐ CREATIVE	☐ SAD
☐ HOPEFUL	☐ STRESSED	☐ TIRED
☐ CALM	☐ ANNOYED	☐ SCARED
☐ ANGRY	☐ POSITIVE	☐ JOYFUL
☐ OVERWHELMED	☐ ANXIOUS	☐ ....

WHO CAN I CONNECT WITH THAT I MISS?

....

....

....

WINS FOR THE DAY

TODAY I ACCOMPLISHED . . .

....

....

....

....

MY THOUGHTS & NOTES

....

....

....

....

....

MORNING INTENTIONS

DATE: .... /........ /........

Think good thoughts. Say nice things. Do good for others. Everything comes back. @powerofpositivity

---

I FEEL . . . I WANT TO FEEL ....

GRATITUDE CHECK

TODAY I AM GRATEFUL FOR . . .

1. ....
2. ....
3. ....

IMAGINE TODAY'S THEME IS COURAGE. DO ONE THING THAT YOU'VE BEEN MEANING TO DO AND EXERCISE YOUR BRAVE MUSCLES. YOU CAN DO ANYTHING!

DAILY AFFIRMATIONS

1. ....
2. ....
3. ....

Bonus: Read each affirmation 10x in the mirror & throughout the day for faster results.

3 PRIORITY GOALS

1. ....
2. ....
3. ....

Self Care Check

- ☐ **PHYSICAL** Rest & recharge.
- ☐ **SOCIAL** Quality conversation.
- ☐ **SPIRITUAL** Good for the soul.
- ☐ **HOUSEHOLD** Cleaning or organizing.
- ☐ **PAMPERING** Treat yourself.
- ☐ **PERSONAL** Time on a hobby.
- ☐ **EMOTIONAL** Honor feelings.
- ☐ **MENTAL** Read or learn.

MY THOUGHTS & NOTES

....

....

....

....

....

EVENING REFLECTIONS

DATE: .... / .... / ....

All things, whatsoever you shall ask in prayer, believing, you shall receive. —Matthew 21:22

GRATITUDE CHECK

TONIGHT I AM GRATEFUL FOR . . .

1. ....

2. ....

3. ....

Wellness Check

☐ **WORKOUT** ☐ **NATURE**

☐ **MEDITATION** **CAFFEINE:** ....

☐ **NUTRITION** **STEPS:** ....

WATER INTAKE:

MENTAL HEALTH CHECK

RIGHT NOW I FEEL . . . (YOU MAY CHOOSE MORE THAN ONE)

☐ HAPPY	☐ PEACEFUL	☐ PROUD
☐ LOVING	☐ CREATIVE	☐ SAD
☐ HOPEFUL	☐ STRESSED	☐ TIRED
☐ CALM	☐ ANNOYED	☐ SCARED
☐ ANGRY	☐ POSITIVE	☐ JOYFUL
☐ OVERWHELMED	☐ ANXIOUS	☐ ....

WHAT CAN I DO FOR MYSELF THAT'S EXTRA SPECIAL?

....

....

....

WINS FOR THE DAY

TODAY I ACCOMPLISHED . . .

....

....

....

....

MY THOUGHTS & NOTES

....

....

....

....

....

MORNING INTENTIONS

DATE: .... /........ /........

Change the way you look at things, and the things you look at change.
—Wayne Dyer

I FEEL . . . I WANT TO FEEL ....

GRATITUDE CHECK

TODAY I AM GRATEFUL FOR . . .

1. ....
2. ....
3. ....

TODAY IS ABOUT CONNECTION! DO ONE THING TODAY THAT BRINGS LOVED ONES TOGETHER.

DAILY AFFIRMATIONS

1. ....
2. ....
3. ....

Bonus: Read each affirmation 10x in the mirror & throughout the day for faster results.

3 PRIORITY GOALS

1. ....
2. ....
3. ....

Self Care Check

- ☐ **PHYSICAL** Rest & recharge.
- ☐ **SOCIAL** Quality conversation.
- ☐ **SPIRITUAL** Good for the soul.
- ☐ **HOUSEHOLD** Cleaning or organizing.
- ☐ **PAMPERING** Treat yourself.
- ☐ **PERSONAL** Time on a hobby.
- ☐ **EMOTIONAL** Honor feelings.
- ☐ **MENTAL** Read or learn.

MY THOUGHTS & NOTES

EVENING REFLECTIONS

DATE: .... /........ /........

We are all faced with great opportunities, brilliantly disguised as impossible situations. —Dr Joe Dispenza joedispenza

---

GRATITUDE CHECK

TONIGHT I AM GRATEFUL FOR . . .

1. ....

2. ....

3. ....

Wellness Check

- ☐ **WORKOUT**
- ☐ **NATURE**
- ☐ **MEDITATION**
- **CAFFEINE:** ....
- ☐ **NUTRITION**
- **STEPS:** ....

WATER INTAKE:

MENTAL HEALTH CHECK

RIGHT NOW I FEEL . . . (YOU MAY CHOOSE MORE THAN ONE)

☐ HAPPY	☐ PEACEFUL	☐ PROUD
☐ LOVING	☐ CREATIVE	☐ SAD
☐ HOPEFUL	☐ STRESSED	☐ TIRED
☐ CALM	☐ ANNOYED	☐ SCARED
☐ ANGRY	☐ POSITIVE	☐ JOYFUL
☐ OVERWHELMED	☐ ANXIOUS	☐ ....

WHAT'S A CYCLE THAT I'VE BEEN EXPERIENCING LATELY? HOW CAN I IMPROVE IT?

....

WINS FOR THE DAY

TODAY I ACCOMPLISHED . . .

....

MY THOUGHTS & NOTES

....

MORNING INTENTIONS

DATE: .... /........ /........

Declare this: Every morning I wake up I am stronger than I was yesterday. @powerofpositivity

I FEEL . . . I WANT TO FEEL ....

GRATITUDE CHECK

TODAY I AM GRATEFUL FOR . . .

1. ....
2. ....
3. ....

DO YOU FEEL WORTHY? IF YOU ANSWERED NO, PLEASE WRITE AND INCLUDE A DAILY AFFIRMATIONS ABOUT SELF-ESTEEM.

DAILY AFFIRMATIONS

1. ....
2. ....
3. ....

Bonus: Read each affirmation 10x in the mirror & throughout the day for faster results.

3 PRIORITY GOALS

1. ....
2. ....
3. ....

Self Care Check

- ☐ **PHYSICAL** Rest & recharge.
- ☐ **SOCIAL** Quality conversation.
- ☐ **SPIRITUAL** Good for the soul.
- ☐ **HOUSEHOLD** Cleaning or organizing.
- ☐ **PAMPERING** Treat yourself.
- ☐ **PERSONAL** Time on a hobby.
- ☐ **EMOTIONAL** Honor feelings.
- ☐ **MENTAL** Read or learn.

MY THOUGHTS & NOTES

....

....

....

....

....

EVENING REFLECTIONS

DATE: .... /........ /........

Having a positive attitude is the only key to genuine happiness. @powerofpositivity

GRATITUDE CHECK

TONIGHT I AM GRATEFUL FOR . . .

1. ....

2. ....

3. ....

Wellness Check

☐ **WORKOUT** ☐ **NATURE**

☐ **MEDITATION** **CAFFEINE:** ....

☐ **NUTRITION** **STEPS:** ....

WATER INTAKE:

MENTAL HEALTH CHECK

RIGHT NOW I FEEL . . . (YOU MAY CHOOSE MORE THAN ONE)

☐ HAPPY	☐ PEACEFUL	☐ PROUD
☐ LOVING	☐ CREATIVE	☐ SAD
☐ HOPEFUL	☐ STRESSED	☐ TIRED
☐ CALM	☐ ANNOYED	☐ SCARED
☐ ANGRY	☐ POSITIVE	☐ JOYFUL
☐ OVERWHELMED	☐ ANXIOUS	☐ ....

WHAT DO YOU WANT TO REMEMBER ABOUT THIS TIME IN YOUR LIFE?

....

....

....

WINS FOR THE DAY

TODAY I ACCOMPLISHED . . .

....

....

....

....

MY THOUGHTS & NOTES

....

....

....

....

....

MORNING INTENTIONS

DATE: .... /........ /........

The most important words you say in your life are the words you say to yourself. —Marisa Peer marisapeertherapy

I FEEL . . . I WANT TO FEEL ....

GRATITUDE CHECK

TODAY I AM GRATEFUL FOR . . .

1. ....
2. ....
3. ....

SMILE CHALLENGE. SMILE AT EVERYONE. IT'S OKAY IF THEY DON'T SMILE BACK, YOU MAY HAVE SILENTLY MADE THEM FEEL GOOD.

DAILY AFFIRMATIONS

1. ....
2. ....
3. ....

Bonus: Read each affirmation 10x in the mirror & throughout the day for faster results.

3 PRIORITY GOALS

1. ....
2. ....
3. ....

Self Care Check

- ☐ **PHYSICAL** Rest & recharge.
- ☐ **SOCIAL** Quality conversation.
- ☐ **SPIRITUAL** Good for the soul.
- ☐ **HOUSEHOLD** Cleaning or organizing.
- ☐ **PAMPERING** Treat yourself.
- ☐ **PERSONAL** Time on a hobby.
- ☐ **EMOTIONAL** Honor feelings.
- ☐ **MENTAL** Read or learn.

MY THOUGHTS & NOTES

EVENING REFLECTIONS

DATE: .... /........ /........

Life is a lottery that we've already won. But most people have not cashed in their tickets. —Louise Hay

GRATITUDE CHECK

TONIGHT I AM GRATEFUL FOR . . .

1. ....

2. ....

3. ....

Wellness Check

- ☐ **WORKOUT**
- ☐ **NATURE**
- ☐ **MEDITATION**
- **CAFFEINE**: ....
- ☐ **NUTRITION**
- **STEPS**: ....

WATER INTAKE:

MENTAL HEALTH CHECK

RIGHT NOW I FEEL . . . (YOU MAY CHOOSE MORE THAN ONE)

☐ HAPPY	☐ PEACEFUL	☐ PROUD
☐ LOVING	☐ CREATIVE	☐ SAD
☐ HOPEFUL	☐ STRESSED	☐ TIRED
☐ CALM	☐ ANNOYED	☐ SCARED
☐ ANGRY	☐ POSITIVE	☐ JOYFUL
☐ OVERWHELMED	☐ ANXIOUS	☐ ....

WHAT DO YOU WANT TO FOCUS ON MOST TOMORROW?

WINS FOR THE DAY

TODAY I ACCOMPLISHED . . .

MY THOUGHTS & NOTES

MORNING INTENTIONS

DATE: .... /........ /........

You can go from underestimated to unstoppable. Step one is to believe.
—Jamie Kern Lima @jamiekernlima

I FEEL . . . I WANT TO FEEL ....

GRATITUDE CHECK

TODAY I AM GRATEFUL FOR . . .

1. ....
2. ....
3. ....

MAKE TODAY A RANDOM ACT OF KINDNESS KINDA DAY! WHAT CAN YOU DO TODAY TO MAKE A RIPPLE EFFECT OF POSITIVITY?

DAILY AFFIRMATIONS

1. ....
2. ....
3. ....

Bonus: Read each affirmation 10x in the mirror & throughout the day for faster results.

3 PRIORITY GOALS

1. ....
2. ....
3. ....

Self Care Check

- ☐ **PHYSICAL** Rest & recharge.
- ☐ **SOCIAL** Quality conversation.
- ☐ **SPIRITUAL** Good for the soul.
- ☐ **HOUSEHOLD** Cleaning or organizing.
- ☐ **PAMPERING** Treat yourself.
- ☐ **PERSONAL** Time on a hobby.
- ☐ **EMOTIONAL** Honor feelings.
- ☐ **MENTAL** Read or learn.

MY THOUGHTS & NOTES

....

....

....

....

....

EVENING REFLECTIONS

DATE: .... / .... / ....

I am not what happened to me, I am what I choose to become.
—Carl Jung

GRATITUDE CHECK

TONIGHT I AM GRATEFUL FOR . . .

1. ....

2. ....

3. ....

Wellness Check

- ☐ **WORKOUT**
- ☐ **NATURE**
- ☐ **MEDITATION**
- **CAFFEINE:** ....
- ☐ **NUTRITION**
- **STEPS:** ....

WATER INTAKE:

MENTAL HEALTH CHECK

RIGHT NOW I FEEL . . . (YOU MAY CHOOSE MORE THAN ONE)

☐ HAPPY	☐ PEACEFUL	☐ PROUD
☐ LOVING	☐ CREATIVE	☐ SAD
☐ HOPEFUL	☐ STRESSED	☐ TIRED
☐ CALM	☐ ANNOYED	☐ SCARED
☐ ANGRY	☐ POSITIVE	☐ JOYFUL
☐ OVERWHELMED	☐ ANXIOUS	☐ ....

WHAT'S SOMETHING YOU'D LIKE TO GET BETTER AT?

....

....

....

WINS FOR THE DAY

TODAY I ACCOMPLISHED . . .

....

....

....

....

MY THOUGHTS & NOTES

....

....

....

....

....

MORNING INTENTIONS

DATE: .... /........ /........

The future depends on what you do today. —Mahatma Gandhi

I FEEL . . . I WANT TO FEEL ....

GRATITUDE CHECK

TODAY I AM GRATEFUL FOR . . .

1. ....
2. ....
3. ....

THINK ABOUT 3 PEOPLE WHO BOTHERED YOU THIS WEEK. SEND THEM LOVE. FORGIVE THEM IN YOUR MIND IF THEY UPSET YOU.

DAILY AFFIRMATIONS

1. ....
2. ....
3. ....

Bonus: Read each affirmation 10x in the mirror & throughout the day for faster results.

3 PRIORITY GOALS

1. ....
2. ....
3. ....

Self Care Check

- ☐ **PHYSICAL** Rest & recharge.
- ☐ **SOCIAL** Quality conversation.
- ☐ **SPIRITUAL** Good for the soul.
- ☐ **HOUSEHOLD** Cleaning or organizing.
- ☐ **PAMPERING** Treat yourself.
- ☐ **PERSONAL** Time on a hobby.
- ☐ **EMOTIONAL** Honor feelings.
- ☐ **MENTAL** Read or learn.

MY THOUGHTS & NOTES

....

....

....

....

....

EVENING REFLECTIONS

DATE: .... /........ /........

It's not about where you're at. It's about what you're doing about where you're at. —Vex King @vexking

GRATITUDE CHECK

TONIGHT I AM GRATEFUL FOR . . .

1. ....

2. ....

3. ....

Wellness Check

- ☐ **WORKOUT**
- ☐ **NATURE**
- ☐ **MEDITATION**
- **CAFFEINE:** ....
- ☐ **NUTRITION**
- **STEPS:** ....

WATER INTAKE:

MENTAL HEALTH CHECK

RIGHT NOW I FEEL . . . (YOU MAY CHOOSE MORE THAN ONE)

☐ HAPPY	☐ PEACEFUL	☐ PROUD
☐ LOVING	☐ CREATIVE	☐ SAD
☐ HOPEFUL	☐ STRESSED	☐ TIRED
☐ CALM	☐ ANNOYED	☐ SCARED
☐ ANGRY	☐ POSITIVE	☐ JOYFUL
☐ OVERWHELMED	☐ ANXIOUS	☐ ....

THE BEST ADVICE I'VE EVER RECEIVED IS . . .

....

....

....

WINS FOR THE DAY

TODAY I ACCOMPLISHED . . .

....

....

....

....

MY THOUGHTS & NOTES

....

....

....

....

....

MORNING INTENTIONS

DATE: .... /........ /........

Your reality is what you choose to believe it is and it will be true for you. —Kristen Butler @positivekristen

I FEEL . . . I WANT TO FEEL ....

GRATITUDE CHECK

TODAY I AM GRATEFUL FOR . . .

1. ....
2. ....
3. ....

THINK OF ALL THE NICE WORDS YOUR BEST FRIEND WOULD USE TO DESCRIBE YOU. WRITE THEM IN TODAY'S NOTES IF YOU WANT. (READ THIS LIST ANYTIME YOU NEED A BOOST.)

DAILY AFFIRMATIONS

1. ....
2. ....
3. ....

Bonus: Read each affirmation 10x in the mirror & throughout the day for faster results.

3 PRIORITY GOALS

1. ....
2. ....
3. ....

Self Care Check

- ☐ **PHYSICAL** Rest & recharge.
- ☐ **SOCIAL** Quality conversation.
- ☐ **SPIRITUAL** Good for the soul.
- ☐ **HOUSEHOLD** Cleaning or organizing.
- ☐ **PAMPERING** Treat yourself.
- ☐ **PERSONAL** Time on a hobby.
- ☐ **EMOTIONAL** Honor feelings.
- ☐ **MENTAL** Read or learn.

MY THOUGHTS & NOTES

....

....

....

....

....

EVENING REFLECTIONS

DATE: .... /........ /........

See the negative. Understand it. Release it. Think positive. Be positive. Speak kindly. Send out good vibes. @powerofpositivity

GRATITUDE CHECK

TONIGHT I AM GRATEFUL FOR . . .

1. ....

2. ....

3. ....

Wellness Check

- ☐ **WORKOUT**
- ☐ **NATURE**
- ☐ **MEDITATION**
- **CAFFEINE:** ....
- ☐ **NUTRITION**
- **STEPS:** ....

WATER INTAKE:

MENTAL HEALTH CHECK

RIGHT NOW I FEEL . . . (YOU MAY CHOOSE MORE THAN ONE)

☐ HAPPY	☐ PEACEFUL	☐ PROUD
☐ LOVING	☐ CREATIVE	☐ SAD
☐ HOPEFUL	☐ STRESSED	☐ TIRED
☐ CALM	☐ ANNOYED	☐ SCARED
☐ ANGRY	☐ POSITIVE	☐ JOYFUL
☐ OVERWHELMED	☐ ANXIOUS	☐ ....

WHAT IS TRULY WORTH FOCUSING ON TODAY? WHAT IS NOT?

....

....

....

WINS FOR THE DAY

TODAY I ACCOMPLISHED . . .

....

....

....

....

MY THOUGHTS & NOTES

....

....

....

....

....

MORNING INTENTIONS

DATE: .... /........ /........

We can build anything in our imagination. That's where all creation begins in your life. —Bob Proctor @proctorgallagher

I FEEL . . . I WANT TO FEEL ....

GRATITUDE CHECK

TODAY I AM GRATEFUL FOR . . .

1. ....
2. ....
3. ....

IMAGINE IT'S YOUR BIRTHDAY TODAY, IF YOU COULD MAKE A WISH WHAT WOULD IT BE? FEEL THE FEELING AS IF THE WISH WAS FULFILLED.

DAILY AFFIRMATIONS

1. ....
2. ....
3. ....

Bonus: Read each affirmation 10x in the mirror & throughout the day for faster results.

3 PRIORITY GOALS

1. ....
2. ....
3. ....

Self Care Check

- ☐ **PHYSICAL** Rest & recharge.
- ☐ **SOCIAL** Quality conversation.
- ☐ **SPIRITUAL** Good for the soul.
- ☐ **HOUSEHOLD** Cleaning or organizing.
- ☐ **PAMPERING** Treat yourself.
- ☐ **PERSONAL** Time on a hobby.
- ☐ **EMOTIONAL** Honor feelings.
- ☐ **MENTAL** Read or learn.

MY THOUGHTS & NOTES

....

....

....

....

....

EVENING REFLECTIONS

DATE: .... / .... / ....

Be still. Good things are here. Feel them. —Kristen Butler
@positivekristen

GRATITUDE CHECK

TONIGHT I AM GRATEFUL FOR . . .

1. ....

2. ....

3. ....

Wellness Check

☐ WORKOUT ☐ NATURE

☐ MEDITATION CAFFEINE: ....

☐ NUTRITION STEPS: ....

WATER INTAKE:

MENTAL HEALTH CHECK

RIGHT NOW I FEEL . . . (YOU MAY CHOOSE MORE THAN ONE)

☐ HAPPY
☐ LOVING
☐ HOPEFUL
☐ CALM
☐ ANGRY
☐ OVERWHELMED
☐ PEACEFUL
☐ CREATIVE
☐ STRESSED
☐ ANNOYED
☐ POSITIVE
☐ ANXIOUS
☐ PROUD
☐ SAD
☐ TIRED
☐ SCARED
☐ JOYFUL
☐ ....

WERE YOU TRUE TO YOURSELF TODAY? WHY OR WHY NOT?

....

WINS FOR THE DAY

TODAY I ACCOMPLISHED . . .

....

MY THOUGHTS & NOTES

....

MORNING INTENTIONS

DATE: .... /........ /........

What lies behind us and what lies before us are tiny matters compared to what lies within us. —Ralph Waldo Emerson

I FEEL . . . I WANT TO FEEL ....

GRATITUDE CHECK

TODAY I AM GRATEFUL FOR . . .

1. ....
2. ....
3. ....

START A CYCLE OF ENCOURAGEMENT. TELL SOMEONE NEAR YOU WHAT YOU APPRECIATE ABOUT THEM.

DAILY AFFIRMATIONS

1. ....
2. ....
3. ....

Bonus: Read each affirmation 10x in the mirror & throughout the day for faster results.

3 PRIORITY GOALS

1. ....
2. ....
3. ....

Self Care Check

- ☐ **PHYSICAL** Rest & recharge.
- ☐ **SOCIAL** Quality conversation.
- ☐ **SPIRITUAL** Good for the soul.
- ☐ **HOUSEHOLD** Cleaning or organizing.
- ☐ **PAMPERING** Treat yourself.
- ☐ **PERSONAL** Time on a hobby.
- ☐ **EMOTIONAL** Honor feelings.
- ☐ **MENTAL** Read or learn.

MY THOUGHTS & NOTES

....

....

....

....

....

EVENING REFLECTIONS

DATE: .... /........ /........

Love is the greatest miracle cure. Loving ourselves works miracles in our lives. —Louise Hay

GRATITUDE CHECK

TONIGHT I AM GRATEFUL FOR . . .

1. ....

2. ....

3. ....

Wellness Check

☐ **WORKOUT** ☐ **NATURE**

☐ **MEDITATION** **CAFFEINE:** ....

☐ **NUTRITION** **STEPS:** ....

WATER INTAKE:

MENTAL HEALTH CHECK

RIGHT NOW I FEEL . . . (YOU MAY CHOOSE MORE THAN ONE)

☐ HAPPY ☐ PEACEFUL ☐ PROUD
☐ LOVING ☐ CREATIVE ☐ SAD
☐ HOPEFUL ☐ STRESSED ☐ TIRED
☐ CALM ☐ ANNOYED ☐ SCARED
☐ ANGRY ☐ POSITIVE ☐ JOYFUL
☐ OVERWHELMED ☐ ANXIOUS ☐ ....

WHAT IS ONE THING I CAN DO TO REDUCE STRESS IN MY LIFE?

....

....

....

WINS FOR THE DAY

TODAY I ACCOMPLISHED . . .

....

....

....

....

MY THOUGHTS & NOTES

....

....

....

....

....

MORNING INTENTIONS

DATE: .... / .... / ....

Believe that every experience you have, even the challenges, is for your growth. @powerofpositivity

I FEEL . . . I WANT TO FEEL ....

GRATITUDE CHECK

TODAY I AM GRATEFUL FOR . . .

1. ....
2. ....
3. ....

CHECK IN WITH YOURSELF A FEW TIMES TODAY AND TAKE A MOMENT TO PROCESS YOUR THOUGHTS AND EMOTIONS. DON'T LET THEM BUILD UP.

DAILY AFFIRMATIONS

1. ....
2. ....
3. ....

Bonus: Read each affirmation 10x in the mirror & throughout the day for faster results.

3 PRIORITY GOALS

1. ....
2. ....
3. ....

Self Care Check

☐ **PHYSICAL**
Rest & recharge.

☐ **SOCIAL**
Quality conversation.

☐ **SPIRITUAL**
Good for the soul.

☐ **HOUSEHOLD**
Cleaning or organizing.

☐ **PAMPERING**
Treat yourself.

☐ **PERSONAL**
Time on a hobby.

☐ **EMOTIONAL**
Honor feelings.

☐ **MENTAL**
Read or learn.

MY THOUGHTS & NOTES

EVENING REFLECTIONS

DATE: .... / .... / ....

Sunsets are proof that no matter what happens, every day can end beautifully. —Kristen Butler @positivekristen

---

GRATITUDE CHECK

TONIGHT I AM GRATEFUL FOR . . .

1. ....

2. ....

3. ....

Wellness Check

☐ **WORKOUT** ☐ **NATURE**

☐ **MEDITATION** **CAFFEINE:** ....

☐ **NUTRITION** **STEPS:** ....

WATER INTAKE:

MENTAL HEALTH CHECK

RIGHT NOW I FEEL . . . (YOU MAY CHOOSE MORE THAN ONE)

☐ HAPPY	☐ PEACEFUL	☐ PROUD
☐ LOVING	☐ CREATIVE	☐ SAD
☐ HOPEFUL	☐ STRESSED	☐ TIRED
☐ CALM	☐ ANNOYED	☐ SCARED
☐ ANGRY	☐ POSITIVE	☐ JOYFUL
☐ OVERWHELMED	☐ ANXIOUS	☐ ....

WHAT MAKES YOUR LIFE SPECIAL RIGHT NOW?

....

....

....

WINS FOR THE DAY

TODAY I ACCOMPLISHED . . .

....

....

....

....

MY THOUGHTS & NOTES

....

....

....

....

....

MORNING INTENTIONS

DATE: .... / .... / ....

The future belongs to those who believe in the beauty of their dreams. —Eleanor Roosevelt

---

I FEEL . . . I WANT TO FEEL ....

GRATITUDE CHECK

TODAY I AM GRATEFUL FOR . . .

1. ....
2. ....
3. ....

WRITE SOMETHING ENCOURAGING ON A POST-IT AND PUT IT WHERE YOU WILL SEE IT EVERY DAY.

DAILY AFFIRMATIONS

1. ....
2. ....
3. ....

Bonus: Read each affirmation 10x in the mirror & throughout the day for faster results.

3 PRIORITY GOALS

1. ....
2. ....
3. ....

Self Care Check

- ☐ **PHYSICAL** Rest & recharge.
- ☐ **SOCIAL** Quality conversation.
- ☐ **SPIRITUAL** Good for the soul.
- ☐ **HOUSEHOLD** Cleaning or organizing.
- ☐ **PAMPERING** Treat yourself.
- ☐ **PERSONAL** Time on a hobby.
- ☐ **EMOTIONAL** Honor feelings.
- ☐ **MENTAL** Read or learn.

MY THOUGHTS & NOTES

....

....

....

....

....

EVENING REFLECTIONS

DATE: .... /........ /........

When you live from a grateful heart, everything you "have to" do starts to shift into things you "get to" do. @positivekristen

GRATITUDE CHECK

TONIGHT I AM GRATEFUL FOR . . .

1. ....

2. ....

3. ....

Wellness Check

☐ **WORKOUT** ☐ **NATURE**

☐ **MEDITATION** **CAFFEINE:** ....

☐ **NUTRITION** **STEPS:** ....

WATER INTAKE:

MENTAL HEALTH CHECK

RIGHT NOW I FEEL . . . (YOU MAY CHOOSE MORE THAN ONE)

☐ HAPPY	☐ PEACEFUL	☐ PROUD
☐ LOVING	☐ CREATIVE	☐ SAD
☐ HOPEFUL	☐ STRESSED	☐ TIRED
☐ CALM	☐ ANNOYED	☐ SCARED
☐ ANGRY	☐ POSITIVE	☐ JOYFUL
☐ OVERWHELMED	☐ ANXIOUS	☐ ....

WHEN WAS THE LAST TIME YOU TRIED SOMETHING NEW? WHAT WAS IT AND HOW DID IT MAKE YOU FEEL?

WINS FOR THE DAY

TODAY I ACCOMPLISHED . . .

MY THOUGHTS & NOTES

MORNING INTENTIONS

DATE: .... /........ /........

May anything that is bothering you be solved, healed, or released today.
@powerofpositivity

I FEEL . . . I WANT TO FEEL ....

GRATITUDE CHECK

TODAY I AM GRATEFUL FOR . . .

1. ....
2. ....
3. ....

DETOX YOUR SOCIAL MEDIA TO GET RID OF ANYTHING THAT MIGHT BE HARMING YOUR MENTAL HEALTH.

DAILY AFFIRMATIONS

1. ....
2. ....
3. ....

Bonus: Read each affirmation 10x in the mirror & throughout the day for faster results.

3 PRIORITY GOALS

1. ....
2. ....
3. ....

Self Care Check

- ☐ **PHYSICAL** Rest & recharge.
- ☐ **SOCIAL** Quality conversation.
- ☐ **SPIRITUAL** Good for the soul.
- ☐ **HOUSEHOLD** Cleaning or organizing.
- ☐ **PAMPERING** Treat yourself.
- ☐ **PERSONAL** Time on a hobby.
- ☐ **EMOTIONAL** Honor feelings.
- ☐ **MENTAL** Read or learn.

MY THOUGHTS & NOTES

EVENING REFLECTIONS

DATE: .... /........ /........

You cannot always control what goes on outside. But you can always control what goes on inside. —Wayne Dyer

GRATITUDE CHECK

TONIGHT I AM GRATEFUL FOR . . .

1. ....

2. ....

3. ....

Wellness Check

☐ **WORKOUT** ☐ **NATURE**

☐ **MEDITATION** **CAFFEINE:** ....

☐ **NUTRITION** **STEPS:** ....

WATER INTAKE:

MENTAL HEALTH CHECK

RIGHT NOW I FEEL . . . (YOU MAY CHOOSE MORE THAN ONE)

☐ HAPPY	☐ PEACEFUL	☐ PROUD
☐ LOVING	☐ CREATIVE	☐ SAD
☐ HOPEFUL	☐ STRESSED	☐ TIRED
☐ CALM	☐ ANNOYED	☐ SCARED
☐ ANGRY	☐ POSITIVE	☐ JOYFUL
☐ OVERWHELMED	☐ ANXIOUS	☐ ....

WHAT IF TODAY WAS THE FIRST DAY OF A NEW YEAR, WHAT WOULD YOU START? WHAT WOULD YOU LET GO OF?

....

....

....

WINS FOR THE DAY

TODAY I ACCOMPLISHED . . .

....

....

....

....

MY THOUGHTS & NOTES

....

....

....

....

....

MORNING INTENTIONS

DATE: .... /........ /........

Rest and recovery is just as important as hustle and grind.
—Dave Hollis MrDaveHollis

I FEEL . . . I WANT TO FEEL ....

GRATITUDE CHECK

TODAY I AM GRATEFUL FOR . . .

1. ....
2. ....
3. ....

WATCH A SUNRISE OR SUNSET. START YOUR DAY OR END YOUR NIGHT BY TAKING A MOMENT TO PRACTICE MINDFULNESS.

DAILY AFFIRMATIONS

1. ....
2. ....
3. ....

Bonus: Read each affirmation 10x in the mirror & throughout the day for faster results.

3 PRIORITY GOALS

1. ....
2. ....
3. ....

Self Care Check

- ☐ **PHYSICAL** Rest & recharge.
- ☐ **SOCIAL** Quality conversation.
- ☐ **SPIRITUAL** Good for the soul.
- ☐ **HOUSEHOLD** Cleaning or organizing.
- ☐ **PAMPERING** Treat yourself.
- ☐ **PERSONAL** Time on a hobby.
- ☐ **EMOTIONAL** Honor feelings.
- ☐ **MENTAL** Read or learn.

MY THOUGHTS & NOTES

EVENING REFLECTIONS

DATE: .... /........ /........

Those who don't believe in magic will never find it. —Roald Dahl

GRATITUDE CHECK

TONIGHT I AM GRATEFUL FOR . . .

1. ....

2. ....

3. ....

Wellness Check

☐ **WORKOUT** ☐ **NATURE**

☐ **MEDITATION** **CAFFEINE:** ....

☐ **NUTRITION** **STEPS:** ....

WATER INTAKE:

MENTAL HEALTH CHECK

RIGHT NOW I FEEL . . . (YOU MAY CHOOSE MORE THAN ONE)

☐ HAPPY	☐ PEACEFUL	☐ PROUD
☐ LOVING	☐ CREATIVE	☐ SAD
☐ HOPEFUL	☐ STRESSED	☐ TIRED
☐ CALM	☐ ANNOYED	☐ SCARED
☐ ANGRY	☐ POSITIVE	☐ JOYFUL
☐ OVERWHELMED	☐ ANXIOUS	☐ ....

IMAGINE YOURSELF IN 10 YEARS EXACTLY THE WAY YOU WANT TO SEE YOURSELF. NOW WRITE DOWN WHAT YOU SEE . . .

....

....

....

WINS FOR THE DAY

TODAY I ACCOMPLISHED . . .

....

....

....

....

MY THOUGHTS & NOTES

....

....

....

....

....

MORNING INTENTIONS

DATE: .... /........ /........

If you believe it will work out, you'll see opportunities. If you believe it won't, you will see obstacles. —Wayne Dyer

I FEEL . . . I WANT TO FEEL ....

GRATITUDE CHECK

TODAY I AM GRATEFUL FOR . . .

1. ....
2. ....
3. ....

BRING OUT YOUR INNER ARTIST. JUST 45 MINUTES OF ART SIGNIFICANTLY REDUCES LEVELS OF THE STRESS HORMONE CORTISOL. WHAT CAN YOU CREATE TODAY?

DAILY AFFIRMATIONS

1. ....
2. ....
3. ....

Bonus: Read each affirmation 10x in the mirror & throughout the day for faster results.

3 PRIORITY GOALS

1. ....
2. ....
3. ....

Self Care Check

- ☐ **PHYSICAL** Rest & recharge.
- ☐ **SOCIAL** Quality conversation.
- ☐ **SPIRITUAL** Good for the soul.
- ☐ **HOUSEHOLD** Cleaning or organizing.
- ☐ **PAMPERING** Treat yourself.
- ☐ **PERSONAL** Time on a hobby.
- ☐ **EMOTIONAL** Honor feelings.
- ☐ **MENTAL** Read or learn.

MY THOUGHTS & NOTES

....

....

....

....

....

EVENING REFLECTIONS

DATE: .... /........ /........

You are not here to make others understand you. You are here to understand yourself. @positivekristen

GRATITUDE CHECK

TONIGHT I AM GRATEFUL FOR . . .

1. ....

2. ....

3. ....

Wellness Check

- ☐ **WORKOUT**
- ☐ **NATURE**
- ☐ **MEDITATION**
- **CAFFEINE:** ....
- ☐ **NUTRITION**
- **STEPS:** ....

WATER INTAKE:

MENTAL HEALTH CHECK

RIGHT NOW I FEEL . . . (YOU MAY CHOOSE MORE THAN ONE)

☐ HAPPY	☐ PEACEFUL	☐ PROUD
☐ LOVING	☐ CREATIVE	☐ SAD
☐ HOPEFUL	☐ STRESSED	☐ TIRED
☐ CALM	☐ ANNOYED	☐ SCARED
☐ ANGRY	☐ POSITIVE	☐ JOYFUL
☐ OVERWHELMED	☐ ANXIOUS	☐ ....

WHAT IS ONE THING THAT MAKES YOU FEEL YOUR BEST?

....

....

....

WINS FOR THE DAY

TODAY I ACCOMPLISHED . . .

....

....

....

....

MY THOUGHTS & NOTES

....

....

....

....

....

MORNING INTENTIONS

DATE: .... /........ /........

Remember, no one has ever achieved anything truly great without going through extreme adversity. —Lewis Howes @lewishowes

I FEEL . . . I WANT TO FEEL ....

GRATITUDE CHECK

TODAY I AM GRATEFUL FOR . . .

1. ....
2. ....
3. ....

PAY ATTENTION TO SOMETHING YOU USUALLY DO ON AUTOPILOT, PERHAPS BRUSHING YOUR TEETH, DRIVING, EATING, OR PERFORMING YOUR MORNING ROUTINE.

DAILY AFFIRMATIONS

1. ....
2. ....
3. ....

Bonus: Read each affirmation 10x in the mirror & throughout the day for faster results.

3 PRIORITY GOALS

1. ....
2. ....
3. ....

Self Care Check

- ☐ **PHYSICAL** Rest & recharge.
- ☐ **SOCIAL** Quality conversation.
- ☐ **SPIRITUAL** Good for the soul.
- ☐ **HOUSEHOLD** Cleaning or organizing.
- ☐ **PAMPERING** Treat yourself.
- ☐ **PERSONAL** Time on a hobby.
- ☐ **EMOTIONAL** Honor feelings.
- ☐ **MENTAL** Read or learn.

MY THOUGHTS & NOTES

....

EVENING REFLECTIONS

DATE: .... /........ /........

Beautiful things happen when you heal and distance yourself from all the negativity and drama. @powerofpositivity

GRATITUDE CHECK

TONIGHT I AM GRATEFUL FOR . . .

1. ....

2. ....

3. ....

Wellness Check

- ☐ **WORKOUT**
- ☐ **NATURE**
- ☐ **MEDITATION**
- **CAFFEINE:** ....
- ☐ **NUTRITION**
- **STEPS:** ....

WATER INTAKE:

MENTAL HEALTH CHECK

RIGHT NOW I FEEL . . . (YOU MAY CHOOSE MORE THAN ONE)

☐ HAPPY	☐ PEACEFUL	☐ PROUD
☐ LOVING	☐ CREATIVE	☐ SAD
☐ HOPEFUL	☐ STRESSED	☐ TIRED
☐ CALM	☐ ANNOYED	☐ SCARED
☐ ANGRY	☐ POSITIVE	☐ JOYFUL
☐ OVERWHELMED	☐ ANXIOUS	☐ ....

DO YOU FEEL OPTIMISTIC ABOUT THE FUTURE? WHY?

....

....

....

WINS FOR THE DAY

TODAY I ACCOMPLISHED . . .

....

....

....

....

MY THOUGHTS & NOTES

....

....

....

....

....

MORNING INTENTIONS

DATE: .... / .... / ....

Shoot for the moon. Even if you miss, you'll land among the stars. —Les Brown

I FEEL . . . I WANT TO FEEL ....

GRATITUDE CHECK

TODAY I AM GRATEFUL FOR . . .

1. ....
2. ....
3. ....

RE-READ YOUR AFFIRMATIONS TODAY 10 TIMES IN THE MIRROR AND THROUGHOUT THE DAY. REPETITION IS KEY TO CHANGE! YOU GOT THIS!

DAILY AFFIRMATIONS

1. ....
2. ....
3. ....

Bonus: Read each affirmation 10x in the mirror & throughout the day for faster results.

3 PRIORITY GOALS

1. ....
2. ....
3. ....

Self Care Check

☐ **PHYSICAL** Rest & recharge.

☐ **SOCIAL** Quality conversation.

☐ **SPIRITUAL** Good for the soul.

☐ **HOUSEHOLD** Cleaning or organizing.

☐ **PAMPERING** Treat yourself.

☐ **PERSONAL** Time on a hobby.

☐ **EMOTIONAL** Honor feelings.

☐ **MENTAL** Read or learn.

MY THOUGHTS & NOTES

EVENING REFLECTIONS

DATE: .... /........ /........

Dear mind, please stop overthinking at night. I'm claiming my rest and peace. @powerofpositivity

GRATITUDE CHECK

TONIGHT I AM GRATEFUL FOR . . .

1. ....

2. ....

3. ....

Wellness Check

☐ **WORKOUT** ☐ **NATURE**

☐ **MEDITATION** **CAFFEINE:** ....

☐ **NUTRITION** **STEPS:** ....

WATER INTAKE:

MENTAL HEALTH CHECK

RIGHT NOW I FEEL . . . (YOU MAY CHOOSE MORE THAN ONE)

☐ HAPPY	☐ PEACEFUL	☐ PROUD
☐ LOVING	☐ CREATIVE	☐ SAD
☐ HOPEFUL	☐ STRESSED	☐ TIRED
☐ CALM	☐ ANNOYED	☐ SCARED
☐ ANGRY	☐ POSITIVE	☐ JOYFUL
☐ OVERWHELMED	☐ ANXIOUS	☐ ....

WHAT CAN YOU DO TOMORROW TO BRING IN MORE JOY?

....

....

....

WINS FOR THE DAY

TODAY I ACCOMPLISHED . . .

....

....

....

....

MY THOUGHTS & NOTES

....

....

....

....

....

MORNING INTENTIONS

DATE: .... / .... / ....

If you want to be happy, set a goal that commands your thoughts, liberates your energy, and inspires your hopes. —Andrew Carnegie

I FEEL . . . I WANT TO FEEL ....

GRATITUDE CHECK

TODAY I AM GRATEFUL FOR . . .

1. ....
2. ....
3. ....

USE YOUR COMMUTE FOR A "BEAUTY SCAVENGER HUNT." FIND FIVE UNEXPECTED BEAUTIFUL THINGS ON YOUR WAY TO WORK.

DAILY AFFIRMATIONS

1. ....
2. ....
3. ....

Bonus: Read each affirmation 10x in the mirror & throughout the day for faster results.

3 PRIORITY GOALS

1. ....
2. ....
3. ....

Self Care Check

☐ **PHYSICAL** Rest & recharge.	☐ **SOCIAL** Quality conversation.
☐ **SPIRITUAL** Good for the soul.	☐ **HOUSEHOLD** Cleaning or organizing.
☐ **PAMPERING** Treat yourself.	☐ **PERSONAL** Time on a hobby.
☐ **EMOTIONAL** Honor feelings.	☐ **MENTAL** Read or learn.

MY THOUGHTS & NOTES

....

EVENING REFLECTIONS

DATE: .... /......... /.........

Look at you, so resilient. You've overcome so much. You can do this. Keep going. Believe in yourself! @positivekristen

---

GRATITUDE CHECK

TONIGHT I AM GRATEFUL FOR . . .

1. ....

2. ....

3. ....

Wellness Check

- ☐ **WORKOUT**
- ☐ **NATURE**
- ☐ **MEDITATION**
- **CAFFEINE:** ....
- ☐ **NUTRITION**
- **STEPS:** ....

WATER INTAKE:

MENTAL HEALTH CHECK

RIGHT NOW I FEEL . . . (YOU MAY CHOOSE MORE THAN ONE)

- ☐ HAPPY
- ☐ LOVING
- ☐ HOPEFUL
- ☐ CALM
- ☐ ANGRY
- ☐ OVERWHELMED
- ☐ PEACEFUL
- ☐ CREATIVE
- ☐ STRESSED
- ☐ ANNOYED
- ☐ POSITIVE
- ☐ ANXIOUS
- ☐ PROUD
- ☐ SAD
- ☐ TIRED
- ☐ SCARED
- ☐ JOYFUL
- ☐ ....

IF YOU COULD CHANGE ONE HABIT, WHAT WOULD IT BE?

....

....

....

WINS FOR THE DAY

TODAY I ACCOMPLISHED . . .

....

....

....

....

MY THOUGHTS & NOTES

....

....

....

....

....

MORNING INTENTIONS

DATE: .... /........ /........

Self-love is a quiet, repeated effort of caring for your soul in a way no one else knows how. dreamdove.talks

I FEEL . . . I WANT TO FEEL ....

GRATITUDE CHECK

TODAY I AM GRATEFUL FOR . . .

1. ....
2. ....
3. ....

ALLOW YOURSELF TO BE PERFECTLY IMPERFECT TODAY. DON'T BEAT YOURSELF UP ABOUT ANYTHING.

DAILY AFFIRMATIONS

1. ....
2. ....
3. ....

Bonus: Read each affirmation 10x in the mirror & throughout the day for faster results.

3 PRIORITY GOALS

1. ....
2. ....
3. ....

Self Care Check

- ☐ **PHYSICAL** Rest & recharge.
- ☐ **SOCIAL** Quality conversation.
- ☐ **SPIRITUAL** Good for the soul.
- ☐ **HOUSEHOLD** Cleaning or organizing.
- ☐ **PAMPERING** Treat yourself.
- ☐ **PERSONAL** Time on a hobby.
- ☐ **EMOTIONAL** Honor feelings.
- ☐ **MENTAL** Read or learn.

MY THOUGHTS & NOTES

EVENING REFLECTIONS

DATE: .... / .... / ....

At the end of the day, all you really need is someone who loves you and always has your back. —Kristen Butler @positivekristen

GRATITUDE CHECK

TONIGHT I AM GRATEFUL FOR . . .

1. ....

2. ....

3. ....

Wellness Check

- ☐ **WORKOUT**
- ☐ **NATURE**
- ☐ **MEDITATION**
- **CAFFEINE**: ....
- ☐ **NUTRITION**
- **STEPS**: ....

WATER INTAKE:

MENTAL HEALTH CHECK

RIGHT NOW I FEEL . . . (YOU MAY CHOOSE MORE THAN ONE)

- ☐ HAPPY
- ☐ LOVING
- ☐ HOPEFUL
- ☐ CALM
- ☐ ANGRY
- ☐ OVERWHELMED
- ☐ PEACEFUL
- ☐ CREATIVE
- ☐ STRESSED
- ☐ ANNOYED
- ☐ POSITIVE
- ☐ ANXIOUS
- ☐ PROUD
- ☐ SAD
- ☐ TIRED
- ☐ SCARED
- ☐ JOYFUL
- ☐ ....

HOW CAN YOU COMMUNICATE YOUR NEEDS BETTER TO OTHERS?

....

....

....

WINS FOR THE DAY

TODAY I ACCOMPLISHED . . .

....

....

....

....

MY THOUGHTS & NOTES

....

....

....

....

....

MORNING INTENTIONS

DATE: .... /........ /........

A positive attitude gives you power over your circumstances instead of your circumstances having power over you. Joyce Meyer @JoyceMeyer

I FEEL . . . I WANT TO FEEL ....

GRATITUDE CHECK

TODAY I AM GRATEFUL FOR . . .

1. ....
2. ....
3. ....

THINK ABOUT YOUR VALUES. THEY'RE THE COMPASS THAT HELPS YOU MAKE DECISIONS AND LIVE A LIFE THAT'S TRUE TO YOU. ONCE YOU DEFINE THEM, DO YOUR BEST TO ALIGN YOUR LIFE WITH THEM.

DAILY AFFIRMATIONS

1. ....
2. ....
3. ....

Bonus: Read each affirmation 10x in the mirror & throughout the day for faster results.

3 PRIORITY GOALS

1. ....
2. ....
3. ....

Self Care Check

- ☐ **PHYSICAL** Rest & recharge.
- ☐ **SOCIAL** Quality conversation.
- ☐ **SPIRITUAL** Good for the soul.
- ☐ **HOUSEHOLD** Cleaning or organizing.
- ☐ **PAMPERING** Treat yourself.
- ☐ **PERSONAL** Time on a hobby.
- ☐ **EMOTIONAL** Honor feelings.
- ☐ **MENTAL** Read or learn.

MY THOUGHTS & NOTES

....

....

....

....

....

EVENING REFLECTIONS

DATE: .... /........ /........

The best part about your story is that the next page is blank and you get to write it. —Chris Butler

GRATITUDE CHECK

TONIGHT I AM GRATEFUL FOR . . .

1. ....

2. ....

3. ....

Wellness Check

- ☐ **WORKOUT**
- ☐ **NATURE**
- ☐ **MEDITATION**
- **CAFFEINE:** ....
- ☐ **NUTRITION**
- **STEPS:** ....

WATER INTAKE:

MENTAL HEALTH CHECK

RIGHT NOW I FEEL . . . (YOU MAY CHOOSE MORE THAN ONE)

☐ HAPPY	☐ PEACEFUL	☐ PROUD
☐ LOVING	☐ CREATIVE	☐ SAD
☐ HOPEFUL	☐ STRESSED	☐ TIRED
☐ CALM	☐ ANNOYED	☐ SCARED
☐ ANGRY	☐ POSITIVE	☐ JOYFUL
☐ OVERWHELMED	☐ ANXIOUS	☐ ....

WHAT IS THE LAST FILM YOU WATCHED THAT INSPIRED YOU? WHY?

....

....

....

WINS FOR THE DAY

TODAY I ACCOMPLISHED . . .

....

....

....

....

MY THOUGHTS & NOTES

....

....

....

....

....

MORNING INTENTIONS

DATE: .... /........ /........

Spread love everywhere you go. Let no one ever come to you without leaving happier. —Mother Teresa

I FEEL . . . I WANT TO FEEL ....

GRATITUDE CHECK

TODAY I AM GRATEFUL FOR . . .

1. ....
2. ....
3. ....

GO OUTSIDE AND LET THE SUNSHINE DO ITS WORK ON YOU AND YOUR IMMUNE SYSTEM FOR AT LEAST 15 MINUTES. IF YOU CAN, GO BAREFOOT AND FEEL YOUR FEET ON THE GROUND.

DAILY AFFIRMATIONS

1. ....
2. ....
3. ....

Bonus: Read each affirmation 10x in the mirror & throughout the day for faster results.

3 PRIORITY GOALS

1. ....
2. ....
3. ....

Self Care Check

- ☐ **PHYSICAL** Rest & recharge.
- ☐ **SOCIAL** Quality conversation.
- ☐ **SPIRITUAL** Good for the soul.
- ☐ **HOUSEHOLD** Cleaning or organizing.
- ☐ **PAMPERING** Treat yourself.
- ☐ **PERSONAL** Time on a hobby.
- ☐ **EMOTIONAL** Honor feelings.
- ☐ **MENTAL** Read or learn.

MY THOUGHTS & NOTES

....

EVENING REFLECTIONS

DATE: .... /........ /........

The very person you find hard to forgive is the one you need to let go of the most. —Louise Hay

GRATITUDE CHECK

TONIGHT I AM GRATEFUL FOR . . .

1. ....

2. ....

3. ....

Wellness Check

☐ **WORKOUT** ☐ **NATURE**

☐ **MEDITATION** **CAFFEINE:** ....

☐ **NUTRITION** **STEPS:** ....

WATER INTAKE:

MENTAL HEALTH CHECK

RIGHT NOW I FEEL . . . (YOU MAY CHOOSE MORE THAN ONE)

☐ HAPPY	☐ PEACEFUL	☐ PROUD
☐ LOVING	☐ CREATIVE	☐ SAD
☐ HOPEFUL	☐ STRESSED	☐ TIRED
☐ CALM	☐ ANNOYED	☐ SCARED
☐ ANGRY	☐ POSITIVE	☐ JOYFUL
☐ OVERWHELMED	☐ ANXIOUS	☐ ....

IS THERE ANYTHING I NEED TO LET GO OF TODAY BEFORE I GO TO SLEEP?

WINS FOR THE DAY

TODAY I ACCOMPLISHED . . .

MY THOUGHTS & NOTES

MORNING INTENTIONS

DATE: .... /........... /...........

Every day is a fresh start. Wake up with a thankful heart.
—Kristen Butler @positivekristen

I FEEL . . . I WANT TO FEEL ....

GRATITUDE CHECK

TODAY I AM GRATEFUL FOR . . .

1. ....
2. ....
3. ....

FORGIVE SOMEONE IN WRITING WITHOUT GIVING IT TO THEM. WORKING THROUGH COMPLEX EMOTIONS LIKE GRIEF ON PAPER IS OFTEN THE BEST PLACE TO START THE HEALING PROCESS.

DAILY AFFIRMATIONS

1. ....
2. ....
3. ....

Bonus: Read each affirmation 10x in the mirror & throughout the day for faster results.

3 PRIORITY GOALS

1. ....
2. ....
3. ....

Self Care Check

☐ **PHYSICAL** Rest & recharge.
☐ **SOCIAL** Quality conversation.
☐ **SPIRITUAL** Good for the soul.
☐ **HOUSEHOLD** Cleaning or organizing.
☐ **PAMPERING** Treat yourself.
☐ **PERSONAL** Time on a hobby.
☐ **EMOTIONAL** Honor feelings.
☐ **MENTAL** Read or learn.

MY THOUGHTS & NOTES

....

EVENING REFLECTIONS

DATE: .... / .... / ....

Looking for the positives out of any challenge makes a big difference in your life. It creates growth. @powerofpositivity

GRATITUDE CHECK

TONIGHT I AM GRATEFUL FOR . . .

1. ....

2. ....

3. ....

Wellness Check

- ☐ **WORKOUT**
- ☐ **NATURE**
- ☐ **MEDITATION**
- **CAFFEINE:** ....
- ☐ **NUTRITION**
- **STEPS:** ....

WATER INTAKE:

MENTAL HEALTH CHECK

RIGHT NOW I FEEL . . . (YOU MAY CHOOSE MORE THAN ONE)

☐ HAPPY	☐ PEACEFUL	☐ PROUD
☐ LOVING	☐ CREATIVE	☐ SAD
☐ HOPEFUL	☐ STRESSED	☐ TIRED
☐ CALM	☐ ANNOYED	☐ SCARED
☐ ANGRY	☐ POSITIVE	☐ JOYFUL
☐ OVERWHELMED	☐ ANXIOUS	☐ ....

HOW DID I POSITIVELY IMPACT SOMEONE ELSE'S LIFE TODAY?

....

....

....

WINS FOR THE DAY

TODAY I ACCOMPLISHED . . .

....

....

....

....

MY THOUGHTS & NOTES

....

....

....

....

....

MORNING INTENTIONS

DATE: .... /........ /........

If you're brave enough to say goodbye, life will reward you with a new hello. —Paulo Coelho @paulocoelho

I FEEL . . . I WANT TO FEEL ....

GRATITUDE CHECK

TODAY I AM GRATEFUL FOR . . .

1. ....
2. ....
3. ....

LET'S IDENTIFY GROWTH FACTORS. WHAT DID YOU DO DIFFERENTLY WHEN YOU EXPERIENCED PAST GROWTH?

DAILY AFFIRMATIONS

1. ....
2. ....
3. ....

Bonus: Read each affirmation 10x in the mirror & throughout the day for faster results.

3 PRIORITY GOALS

1. ....
2. ....
3. ....

Self Care Check

- ☐ **PHYSICAL** Rest & recharge.
- ☐ **SOCIAL** Quality conversation.
- ☐ **SPIRITUAL** Good for the soul.
- ☐ **HOUSEHOLD** Cleaning or organizing.
- ☐ **PAMPERING** Treat yourself.
- ☐ **PERSONAL** Time on a hobby.
- ☐ **EMOTIONAL** Honor feelings.
- ☐ **MENTAL** Read or learn.

MY THOUGHTS & NOTES

EVENING REFLECTIONS

DATE: .... / .... / ....

Sometimes things fall apart so that better things can fall together.
—Marilyn Monroe

GRATITUDE CHECK

TONIGHT I AM GRATEFUL FOR . . .

1. ....

2. ....

3. ....

Wellness Check

☐ **WORKOUT** ☐ **NATURE**

☐ **MEDITATION** **CAFFEINE:** ....

☐ **NUTRITION** **STEPS:** ....

WATER INTAKE:

MENTAL HEALTH CHECK

RIGHT NOW I FEEL . . . (YOU MAY CHOOSE MORE THAN ONE)

☐ HAPPY	☐ PEACEFUL	☐ PROUD
☐ LOVING	☐ CREATIVE	☐ SAD
☐ HOPEFUL	☐ STRESSED	☐ TIRED
☐ CALM	☐ ANNOYED	☐ SCARED
☐ ANGRY	☐ POSITIVE	☐ JOYFUL
☐ OVERWHELMED	☐ ANXIOUS	☐ ....

WHAT DID I DO TODAY THAT DID NOT BRING ME HAPPINESS? WHY?

....

....

....

WINS FOR THE DAY

TODAY I ACCOMPLISHED . . .

....

....

....

....

MY THOUGHTS & NOTES

....

....

....

....

....

MORNING INTENTIONS

DATE: .... / .... / ....

Challenges can't stop you. People can't stop you. Time can't stop you. Your own negative thoughts can. Stay positive. —Kristen Butler @positivekristen

I FEEL . . . I WANT TO FEEL ....

GRATITUDE CHECK

TODAY I AM GRATEFUL FOR . . .

1. ....
2. ....
3. ....

ARE YOU AFRAID TO MAKE MISTAKES? IF YOU ANSWERED YES, REMEMBER, MISTAKES ARE PROOF THAT YOU ARE TRYING. THE MOST SUCCESSFUL PEOPLE HAVE A LIFE FILLED WITH MISTAKES.

DAILY AFFIRMATIONS

1. ....
2. ....
3. ....

Bonus: Read each affirmation 10x in the mirror & throughout the day for faster results.

3 PRIORITY GOALS

1. ....
2. ....
3. ....

Self Care Check

- ☐ **PHYSICAL** Rest & recharge.
- ☐ **SOCIAL** Quality conversation.
- ☐ **SPIRITUAL** Good for the soul.
- ☐ **HOUSEHOLD** Cleaning or organizing.
- ☐ **PAMPERING** Treat yourself.
- ☐ **PERSONAL** Time on a hobby.
- ☐ **EMOTIONAL** Honor feelings.
- ☐ **MENTAL** Read or learn.

MY THOUGHTS & NOTES

....

....

....

....

....

EVENING REFLECTIONS

DATE: .... /........ /........

A good reminder...No matter how hard your life is, go to bed grateful you still have one. @powerofpositivity

---

GRATITUDE CHECK

TONIGHT I AM GRATEFUL FOR . . .

1. ....

2. ....

3. ....

Wellness Check

- ☐ **WORKOUT**
- ☐ **NATURE**
- ☐ **MEDITATION**
- **CAFFEINE:** ....
- ☐ **NUTRITION**
- **STEPS:** ....

WATER INTAKE:

MENTAL HEALTH CHECK

RIGHT NOW I FEEL . . . (YOU MAY CHOOSE MORE THAN ONE)

☐ HAPPY	☐ PEACEFUL	☐ PROUD
☐ LOVING	☐ CREATIVE	☐ SAD
☐ HOPEFUL	☐ STRESSED	☐ TIRED
☐ CALM	☐ ANNOYED	☐ SCARED
☐ ANGRY	☐ POSITIVE	☐ JOYFUL
☐ OVERWHELMED	☐ ANXIOUS	☐ ....

WHO INSPIRES YOU TO BE A BETTER VERSION OF YOURSELF? WHY?

....

....

....

WINS FOR THE DAY

TODAY I ACCOMPLISHED . . .

....

....

....

....

MY THOUGHTS & NOTES

....

....

....

....

....

MORNING INTENTIONS

DATE: .... /......... /.........

Show up in love for yourself. As you embody that love, you become a magnet to receiving more of it. @theDanetteMay

I FEEL . . . I WANT TO FEEL ....

GRATITUDE CHECK

TODAY I AM GRATEFUL FOR . . .

1. ....
2. ....
3. ....

FOR ONE WEEK, GIVE UP SCREEN USAGE ONE HOUR BEFORE BEDTIME. THERE ARE NUMEROUS ADVANTAGES TO AVOIDING BLUE LIGHT EXPOSURE. YOUR EYES AND MENTAL HEALTH WILL THANK YOU.

DAILY AFFIRMATIONS

1. ....
2. ....
3. ....

Bonus: Read each affirmation 10x in the mirror & throughout the day for faster results.

3 PRIORITY GOALS

1. ....
2. ....
3. ....

Self Care Check

- ☐ **PHYSICAL** Rest & recharge.
- ☐ **SOCIAL** Quality conversation.
- ☐ **SPIRITUAL** Good for the soul.
- ☐ **HOUSEHOLD** Cleaning or organizing.
- ☐ **PAMPERING** Treat yourself.
- ☐ **PERSONAL** Time on a hobby.
- ☐ **EMOTIONAL** Honor feelings.
- ☐ **MENTAL** Read or learn.

MY THOUGHTS & NOTES

....

....

....

....

....

EVENING REFLECTIONS

DATE: .... /........ /........

Be patient. Everything's coming together. Take time to rest.

GRATITUDE CHECK

TONIGHT I AM GRATEFUL FOR . . .

1. ....

2. ....

3. ....

Wellness Check

- ☐ **WORKOUT**
- ☐ **NATURE**
- ☐ **MEDITATION**
- **CAFFEINE:** ....
- ☐ **NUTRITION**
- **STEPS:** ....

WATER INTAKE:

MENTAL HEALTH CHECK

RIGHT NOW I FEEL . . . (YOU MAY CHOOSE MORE THAN ONE)

☐ HAPPY	☐ PEACEFUL	☐ PROUD
☐ LOVING	☐ CREATIVE	☐ SAD
☐ HOPEFUL	☐ STRESSED	☐ TIRED
☐ CALM	☐ ANNOYED	☐ SCARED
☐ ANGRY	☐ POSITIVE	☐ JOYFUL
☐ OVERWHELMED	☐ ANXIOUS	☐ ....

WHAT IS BETTER TODAY THAN IT WAS A YEAR AGO THAT YOU CAN BE GRATEFUL FOR?

....

....

....

WINS FOR THE DAY

TODAY I ACCOMPLISHED . . .

....

....

....

....

MY THOUGHTS & NOTES

....

....

....

....

....

MORNING INTENTIONS

DATE: .... /........ /........

Be kind. Appreciate the little things. Smile. Stay humble. Do good.
@powerofpositivity

I FEEL . . . I WANT TO FEEL ....

GRATITUDE CHECK

TODAY I AM GRATEFUL FOR . . .

1. ....
2. ....
3. ....

DO YOU SEE THE GLASS HALF FULL? LOOK AT EVERYTHING IN YOUR DAY TODAY WITH A POSITIVE MINDSET. EVEN THE TOUGHEST CHALLENGES HAVE A GLIMMER OF HOPE.

DAILY AFFIRMATIONS

1. ....
2. ....
3. ....

Bonus: Read each affirmation 10x in the mirror & throughout the day for faster results.

3 PRIORITY GOALS

1. ....
2. ....
3. ....

Self Care Check

- ☐ **PHYSICAL** Rest & recharge.
- ☐ **SOCIAL** Quality conversation.
- ☐ **SPIRITUAL** Good for the soul.
- ☐ **HOUSEHOLD** Cleaning or organizing.
- ☐ **PAMPERING** Treat yourself.
- ☐ **PERSONAL** Time on a hobby.
- ☐ **EMOTIONAL** Honor feelings.
- ☐ **MENTAL** Read or learn.

MY THOUGHTS & NOTES

....

....

....

....

....

EVENING REFLECTIONS

DATE: .... /........ /........

Stop chasing. Stop forcing. Just flow. Follow your intuition. Let what comes, come and let what goes, go. —Kristen Butler @positivekristen

GRATITUDE CHECK

TONIGHT I AM GRATEFUL FOR . . .

1. ....

2. ....

3. ....

Wellness Check

☐ **WORKOUT** ☐ **NATURE**

☐ **MEDITATION** **CAFFEINE:** ....

☐ **NUTRITION** **STEPS:** ....

WATER INTAKE:

MENTAL HEALTH CHECK

RIGHT NOW I FEEL . . . (YOU MAY CHOOSE MORE THAN ONE)

☐ HAPPY ☐ PEACEFUL ☐ PROUD

☐ LOVING ☐ CREATIVE ☐ SAD

☐ HOPEFUL ☐ STRESSED ☐ TIRED

☐ CALM ☐ ANNOYED ☐ SCARED

☐ ANGRY ☐ POSITIVE ☐ JOYFUL

☐ OVERWHELMED ☐ ANXIOUS ☐ ....

WHAT DID YOU DO CONSISTENTLY TODAY? WHAT DID YOU DO DIFFERENTLY?

....

....

....

WINS FOR THE DAY

TODAY I ACCOMPLISHED . . .

....

....

....

....

MY THOUGHTS & NOTES

....

....

....

....

....

MORNING INTENTIONS

DATE: .... / .... / ....

Stop for a minute, breathe, and be proud of yourself for how far you've come. @powerofpositivity

I FEEL . . . I WANT TO FEEL ....

GRATITUDE CHECK

TODAY I AM GRATEFUL FOR . . .

1. ....
2. ....
3. ....

DO YOU EVER LET YOUR INNER CHILD COME OUT AND PLAY? TODAY, HOLD SPACE FOR THE YOUNGER VERSION OF YOURSELF. DO SOMETHING THAT LETS YOU PLAY, SMILE, LAUGH AND HAVE FUN.

DAILY AFFIRMATIONS

1. ....
2. ....
3. ....

Bonus: Read each affirmation 10x in the mirror & throughout the day for faster results.

3 PRIORITY GOALS

1. ....
2. ....
3. ....

Self Care Check

- ☐ **PHYSICAL** Rest & recharge.
- ☐ **SOCIAL** Quality conversation.
- ☐ **SPIRITUAL** Good for the soul.
- ☐ **HOUSEHOLD** Cleaning or organizing.
- ☐ **PAMPERING** Treat yourself.
- ☐ **PERSONAL** Time on a hobby.
- ☐ **EMOTIONAL** Honor feelings.
- ☐ **MENTAL** Read or learn.

MY THOUGHTS & NOTES

....

....

....

....

....

EVENING REFLECTIONS

DATE: .... / .... / ....

This will pass... and when it does you'll be stronger than you ever thought you could be. —Kristen Butler @positivekristen

---

GRATITUDE CHECK

TONIGHT I AM GRATEFUL FOR . . .

1. ....
2. ....
3. ....

Wellness Check

- ☐ **WORKOUT**
- ☐ **NATURE**
- ☐ **MEDITATION**
- **CAFFEINE:** ....
- ☐ **NUTRITION**
- **STEPS:** ....

WATER INTAKE:

MENTAL HEALTH CHECK

RIGHT NOW I FEEL . . . (YOU MAY CHOOSE MORE THAN ONE)

☐ HAPPY	☐ PEACEFUL	☐ PROUD
☐ LOVING	☐ CREATIVE	☐ SAD
☐ HOPEFUL	☐ STRESSED	☐ TIRED
☐ CALM	☐ ANNOYED	☐ SCARED
☐ ANGRY	☐ POSITIVE	☐ JOYFUL
☐ OVERWHELMED	☐ ANXIOUS	☐ ....

WHAT MADE YOU LAUGH OR SMILE TODAY?

....

....

....

WINS FOR THE DAY

TODAY I ACCOMPLISHED . . .

....

....

....

....

MY THOUGHTS & NOTES

....

....

....

....

....

MORNING INTENTIONS

DATE: .... /......... /.........

If you want to lift yourself up, lift up someone else.
—Booker T. Washington

I FEEL . . . I WANT TO FEEL ....

GRATITUDE CHECK

TODAY I AM GRATEFUL FOR . . .

1. ....
2. ....
3. ....

HOW MANY TIMES DO YOU SAY "YES" TO OTHERS WHEN YOU REALLY WANT TO SAY "NO"? THINK ABOUT HOW YOU CAN HONOR YOUR FEELINGS TODAY.

DAILY AFFIRMATIONS

1. ....
2. ....
3. ....

Bonus: Read each affirmation 10x in the mirror & throughout the day for faster results.

3 PRIORITY GOALS

1. ....
2. ....
3. ....

Self Care Check

- ☐ **PHYSICAL** Rest & recharge.
- ☐ **SOCIAL** Quality conversation.
- ☐ **SPIRITUAL** Good for the soul.
- ☐ **HOUSEHOLD** Cleaning or organizing.
- ☐ **PAMPERING** Treat yourself.
- ☐ **PERSONAL** Time on a hobby.
- ☐ **EMOTIONAL** Honor feelings.
- ☐ **MENTAL** Read or learn.

MY THOUGHTS & NOTES

....

....

....

....

....

EVENING REFLECTIONS

DATE: .... /........ /........

When you continuously spread positive vibes, Karma is naturally rigged in your favor. Life loves authenticity and consistency. —Kristen Butler @positivekristen

GRATITUDE CHECK

TONIGHT I AM GRATEFUL FOR . . .

1. ....

2. ....

3. ....

Wellness Check

- ☐ **WORKOUT**
- ☐ **NATURE**
- ☐ **MEDITATION**
- **CAFFEINE:** ....
- ☐ **NUTRITION**
- **STEPS:** ....

WATER INTAKE:

MENTAL HEALTH CHECK

RIGHT NOW I FEEL . . . (YOU MAY CHOOSE MORE THAN ONE)

☐ HAPPY	☐ PEACEFUL	☐ PROUD
☐ LOVING	☐ CREATIVE	☐ SAD
☐ HOPEFUL	☐ STRESSED	☐ TIRED
☐ CALM	☐ ANNOYED	☐ SCARED
☐ ANGRY	☐ POSITIVE	☐ JOYFUL
☐ OVERWHELMED	☐ ANXIOUS	☐ ....

WHAT'S THE BEST COMPLIMENT YOU CAN GIVE YOURSELF RIGHT NOW?

....

....

....

WINS FOR THE DAY

TODAY I ACCOMPLISHED . . .

....

....

....

....

MY THOUGHTS & NOTES

....

....

....

....

....

MORNING INTENTIONS

DATE: .... / .... / ....

Sometimes I just need a break in a beautiful place, to stop, listen to my heart, and figure it all out. @powerofpositivity

I FEEL . . . I WANT TO FEEL ....

GRATITUDE CHECK

TODAY I AM GRATEFUL FOR . . .

1. ....
2. ....
3. ....

MUSIC HOLDS POWER IN ELEVATING OUR EMOTIONS. TAKE TIME TO LISTEN TO YOUR FAVORITE MUSIC TODAY AND TRULY IMMERSE YOURSELF.

DAILY AFFIRMATIONS

1. ....
2. ....
3. ....

Bonus: Read each affirmation 10x in the mirror & throughout the day for faster results.

3 PRIORITY GOALS

1. ....
2. ....
3. ....

Self Care Check

- ☐ **PHYSICAL** Rest & recharge.
- ☐ **SOCIAL** Quality conversation.
- ☐ **SPIRITUAL** Good for the soul.
- ☐ **HOUSEHOLD** Cleaning or organizing.
- ☐ **PAMPERING** Treat yourself.
- ☐ **PERSONAL** Time on a hobby.
- ☐ **EMOTIONAL** Honor feelings.
- ☐ **MENTAL** Read or learn.

MY THOUGHTS & NOTES

EVENING REFLECTIONS

DATE: .... /........ /........

Courage is not having strength to go on; it's going on when you don't have strength. —Theodore Roosevelt

GRATITUDE CHECK

TONIGHT I AM GRATEFUL FOR . . .

1. ....

2. ....

3. ....

Wellness Check

- ☐ **WORKOUT**
- ☐ **NATURE**
- ☐ **MEDITATION**
- **CAFFEINE**: ....
- ☐ **NUTRITION**
- **STEPS**: ....

WATER INTAKE:

MENTAL HEALTH CHECK

RIGHT NOW I FEEL . . . (YOU MAY CHOOSE MORE THAN ONE)

☐ HAPPY	☐ PEACEFUL	☐ PROUD
☐ LOVING	☐ CREATIVE	☐ SAD
☐ HOPEFUL	☐ STRESSED	☐ TIRED
☐ CALM	☐ ANNOYED	☐ SCARED
☐ ANGRY	☐ POSITIVE	☐ JOYFUL
☐ OVERWHELMED	☐ ANXIOUS	☐ ....

WHAT'S ONE THOUGHTFUL THING SOMEONE DID FOR YOU RECENTLY?

....

....

....

WINS FOR THE DAY

TODAY I ACCOMPLISHED . . .

....

....

....

....

MY THOUGHTS & NOTES

....

....

....

....

....

MORNING INTENTIONS

DATE: .... /........ /........

The smartest thing anyone can ever do is put their self-worth on the top shelf. Kristen Butler @positivekristen

I FEEL . . . I WANT TO FEEL ....

GRATITUDE CHECK

TODAY I AM GRATEFUL FOR . . .

1. ....
2. ....
3. ....

WHEN THINGS GO WRONG DO YOU TEND TO IMMEDIATELY TURN TO A SOLUTION OR DWELL ON THE PROBLEM? TODAY BE MINDFUL OF HOW YOU RESPOND.

DAILY AFFIRMATIONS

1. ....
2. ....
3. ....

Bonus: Read each affirmation 10x in the mirror & throughout the day for faster results.

3 PRIORITY GOALS

1. ....
2. ....
3. ....

Self Care Check

- ☐ **PHYSICAL** Rest & recharge.
- ☐ **SOCIAL** Quality conversation.
- ☐ **SPIRITUAL** Good for the soul.
- ☐ **HOUSEHOLD** Cleaning or organizing.
- ☐ **PAMPERING** Treat yourself.
- ☐ **PERSONAL** Time on a hobby.
- ☐ **EMOTIONAL** Honor feelings.
- ☐ **MENTAL** Read or learn.

MY THOUGHTS & NOTES

....

....

....

....

....

EVENING REFLECTIONS

DATE: .... /........ /........

Sometimes you have to unplug yourself from the world for a moment, so you can reset yourself. —Vex King @vexking

GRATITUDE CHECK

TONIGHT I AM GRATEFUL FOR . . .

1. ....

2. ....

3. ....

Wellness Check

- ☐ **WORKOUT**
- ☐ **NATURE**
- ☐ **MEDITATION**
- **CAFFEINE:** ....
- ☐ **NUTRITION**
- **STEPS:** ....

WATER INTAKE:

MENTAL HEALTH CHECK

RIGHT NOW I FEEL . . . (YOU MAY CHOOSE MORE THAN ONE)

☐ HAPPY	☐ PEACEFUL	☐ PROUD
☐ LOVING	☐ CREATIVE	☐ SAD
☐ HOPEFUL	☐ STRESSED	☐ TIRED
☐ CALM	☐ ANNOYED	☐ SCARED
☐ ANGRY	☐ POSITIVE	☐ JOYFUL
☐ OVERWHELMED	☐ ANXIOUS	☐ ....

WHAT WOULD I HAVE DONE DIFFERENTLY TODAY IF I WEREN'T WORRIED ABOUT BEING JUDGED?

....

....

....

WINS FOR THE DAY

TODAY I ACCOMPLISHED . . .

....

....

....

....

MY THOUGHTS & NOTES

....

....

....

....

....

MORNING INTENTIONS

DATE: .... /........ /........

Today, allow your heart to remain wide open and then pay attention to the love and beautiful synchronicities that are guiding the way. @powerofpositivity

I FEEL . . . I WANT TO FEEL ....

GRATITUDE CHECK

TODAY I AM GRATEFUL FOR . . .

1. ....
2. ....
3. ....

A POSITIVE MINDSET DECREASES CORTISOL LEVELS, WHICH IMPROVES SLEEP, HORMONES, MOTIVATION, AND MORE. IT'S A GAME CHANGER. SHARE THIS FACT WITH SOMEONE ELSE TODAY.

DAILY AFFIRMATIONS

1. ....
2. ....
3. ....

Bonus: Read each affirmation 10x in the mirror & throughout the day for faster results.

3 PRIORITY GOALS

1. ....
2. ....
3. ....

Self Care Check

☐ **PHYSICAL** Rest & recharge.

☐ **SOCIAL** Quality conversation.

☐ **SPIRITUAL** Good for the soul.

☐ **HOUSEHOLD** Cleaning or organizing.

☐ **PAMPERING** Treat yourself.

☐ **PERSONAL** Time on a hobby.

☐ **EMOTIONAL** Honor feelings.

☐ **MENTAL** Read or learn.

MY THOUGHTS & NOTES

....

....

....

....

....

EVENING REFLECTIONS

DATE: .... /........ /........

Your job is to create a vision that makes you want to jump out of bed in the morning. If it doesn't, go back to bed until you have a bigger dream. @lewishowes

---

GRATITUDE CHECK

TONIGHT I AM GRATEFUL FOR . . .

1. ....

2. ....

3. ....

Wellness Check

☐ **WORKOUT** ☐ **NATURE**

☐ **MEDITATION** **CAFFEINE**: ....

☐ **NUTRITION** **STEPS**: ....

WATER INTAKE:

MENTAL HEALTH CHECK

RIGHT NOW I FEEL . . . (YOU MAY CHOOSE MORE THAN ONE)

☐ HAPPY
☐ LOVING
☐ HOPEFUL
☐ CALM
☐ ANGRY
☐ OVERWHELMED
☐ PEACEFUL
☐ CREATIVE
☐ STRESSED
☐ ANNOYED
☐ POSITIVE
☐ ANXIOUS
☐ PROUD
☐ SAD
☐ TIRED
☐ SCARED
☐ JOYFUL
☐ ....

HOW CAN YOU ADD MORE FUN INTO YOUR DAY?

....

....

....

WINS FOR THE DAY

TODAY I ACCOMPLISHED . . .

....

....

....

....

MY THOUGHTS & NOTES

....

....

....

....

....

MORNING INTENTIONS

DATE: .... /........ /........

You must make your dreams a priority in order for it to become your life. —Bob Proctor proctorgallagher

I FEEL . . . I WANT TO FEEL ....

GRATITUDE CHECK

TODAY I AM GRATEFUL FOR . . .

1. ....
2. ....
3. ....

DO YOU HAVE A GRATITUDE JAR? IF NOT, MAKE ONE. USE A MASON JAR AND WRITE YOUR FIRST ONE. PUT IT SOMEWHERE YOU WILL REMEMBER TO USE IT.

DAILY AFFIRMATIONS

1. ....
2. ....
3. ....

Bonus: Read each affirmation 10x in the mirror & throughout the day for faster results.

3 PRIORITY GOALS

1. ....
2. ....
3. ....

Self Care Check

- ☐ **PHYSICAL** Rest & recharge.
- ☐ **SOCIAL** Quality conversation.
- ☐ **SPIRITUAL** Good for the soul.
- ☐ **HOUSEHOLD** Cleaning or organizing.
- ☐ **PAMPERING** Treat yourself.
- ☐ **PERSONAL** Time on a hobby.
- ☐ **EMOTIONAL** Honor feelings.
- ☐ **MENTAL** Read or learn.

MY THOUGHTS & NOTES

....

....

....

....

....

EVENING REFLECTIONS

DATE: .... /......... /.........

The strongest people I've met have not been given an easier life. They've learned to create strength and happiness from dark places. @positivekristen

GRATITUDE CHECK

TONIGHT I AM GRATEFUL FOR . . .

1. ....

2. ....

3. ....

Wellness Check

- ☐ **WORKOUT**
- ☐ **NATURE**
- ☐ **MEDITATION**
- **CAFFEINE:** ....
- ☐ **NUTRITION**
- **STEPS:** ....

WATER INTAKE:

MENTAL HEALTH CHECK

RIGHT NOW I FEEL . . . (YOU MAY CHOOSE MORE THAN ONE)

☐ HAPPY	☐ PEACEFUL	☐ PROUD
☐ LOVING	☐ CREATIVE	☐ SAD
☐ HOPEFUL	☐ STRESSED	☐ TIRED
☐ CALM	☐ ANNOYED	☐ SCARED
☐ ANGRY	☐ POSITIVE	☐ JOYFUL
☐ OVERWHELMED	☐ ANXIOUS	☐ ....

TODAY WAS GREAT BECAUSE . . .

....

....

....

....

WINS FOR THE DAY

TODAY I ACCOMPLISHED . . .

....

....

....

....

MY THOUGHTS & NOTES

....

....

....

....

....

MORNING INTENTIONS

DATE: .... /........ /........

You have been criticizing yourself for years, and it hasn't worked. Try approving of yourself and see what happens. —Louise L. Hay

I FEEL . . . I WANT TO FEEL ....

GRATITUDE CHECK

TODAY I AM GRATEFUL FOR . . .

1. ....
2. ....
3. ....

PHYSICAL TOUCH IS SUCH A GOOD MOOD BOOST. THIS IS YOUR REMINDER TO GIVE MORE HUGS, HOLD HANDS, GIVE HIGH FIVES, OR GET A MASSAGE.

DAILY AFFIRMATIONS

1. ....
2. ....
3. ....

Bonus: Read each affirmation 10x in the mirror & throughout the day for faster results.

3 PRIORITY GOALS

1. ....
2. ....
3. ....

Self Care Check

- ☐ **PHYSICAL** Rest & recharge.
- ☐ **SOCIAL** Quality conversation.
- ☐ **SPIRITUAL** Good for the soul.
- ☐ **HOUSEHOLD** Cleaning or organizing.
- ☐ **PAMPERING** Treat yourself.
- ☐ **PERSONAL** Time on a hobby.
- ☐ **EMOTIONAL** Honor feelings.
- ☐ **MENTAL** Read or learn.

MY THOUGHTS & NOTES

....

....

....

....

....

EVENING REFLECTIONS

DATE: .... / .... / ....

Sometimes all it takes is one prayer or concentrated positive thought to change everything. @powerofpositivity

GRATITUDE CHECK

TONIGHT I AM GRATEFUL FOR . . .

1. ....

2. ....

3. ....

Wellness Check

☐ **WORKOUT** ☐ **NATURE**

☐ **MEDITATION** **CAFFEINE:** ....

☐ **NUTRITION** **STEPS:** ....

WATER INTAKE:

MENTAL HEALTH CHECK

RIGHT NOW I FEEL . . . (YOU MAY CHOOSE MORE THAN ONE)

☐ HAPPY	☐ PEACEFUL	☐ PROUD
☐ LOVING	☐ CREATIVE	☐ SAD
☐ HOPEFUL	☐ STRESSED	☐ TIRED
☐ CALM	☐ ANNOYED	☐ SCARED
☐ ANGRY	☐ POSITIVE	☐ JOYFUL
☐ OVERWHELMED	☐ ANXIOUS	☐ ....

WHAT SPECIFICALLY DO YOU NEED TO FORGIVE YOURSELF FOR?

WINS FOR THE DAY

TODAY I ACCOMPLISHED . . .

MY THOUGHTS & NOTES

MORNING INTENTIONS

DATE: .... /........ /........

Happiness now is happiness tomorrow. Ellie Shoja @braveellie

I FEEL . . . I WANT TO FEEL ....

GRATITUDE CHECK

TODAY I AM GRATEFUL FOR . . .

1. ....
2. ....
3. ....

MINDFUL CONVERSATION IS SO IMPORTANT. WE ARE ABLE TO TAKE TURNS, THINK BEFORE WE SPEAK, ACTIVELY LISTEN, USE INTENTIONAL LANGUAGE, ETC. TRY IT...

DAILY AFFIRMATIONS

1. ....
2. ....
3. ....

Bonus: Read each affirmation 10x in the mirror & throughout the day for faster results.

3 PRIORITY GOALS

1. ....
2. ....
3. ....

Self Care Check

- ☐ **PHYSICAL** Rest & recharge.
- ☐ **SOCIAL** Quality conversation.
- ☐ **SPIRITUAL** Good for the soul.
- ☐ **HOUSEHOLD** Cleaning or organizing.
- ☐ **PAMPERING** Treat yourself.
- ☐ **PERSONAL** Time on a hobby.
- ☐ **EMOTIONAL** Honor feelings.
- ☐ **MENTAL** Read or learn.

MY THOUGHTS & NOTES

EVENING REFLECTIONS

DATE: .... /........ /........

The happiest people do not have the best of everything. They make the best out of everything that comes their way. @powerofpositivity

GRATITUDE CHECK

TONIGHT I AM GRATEFUL FOR . . .

1. ....

2. ....

3. ....

Wellness Check

- ☐ **WORKOUT**
- ☐ **NATURE**
- ☐ **MEDITATION**
- **CAFFEINE:** ....
- ☐ **NUTRITION**
- **STEPS:** ....

WATER INTAKE:

MENTAL HEALTH CHECK

RIGHT NOW I FEEL . . . (YOU MAY CHOOSE MORE THAN ONE)

☐ HAPPY	☐ PEACEFUL	☐ PROUD
☐ LOVING	☐ CREATIVE	☐ SAD
☐ HOPEFUL	☐ STRESSED	☐ TIRED
☐ CALM	☐ ANNOYED	☐ SCARED
☐ ANGRY	☐ POSITIVE	☐ JOYFUL
☐ OVERWHELMED	☐ ANXIOUS	☐ ....

WHAT DO YOU WANT TO REMEMBER ABOUT THIS TIME IN YOUR LIFE?

....

....

....

WINS FOR THE DAY

TODAY I ACCOMPLISHED . . .

....

....

....

....

MY THOUGHTS & NOTES

....

....

....

....

....

MORNING INTENTIONS

DATE: .... /........ /........

If you don't like something, change it. If you can't change it, change your attitude. —Maya Angelou

I FEEL . . . I WANT TO FEEL ....

GRATITUDE CHECK

TODAY I AM GRATEFUL FOR . . .

1. ....
2. ....
3. ....

NO HIDING TODAY. BE UNAPOLOGETICALLY YOU. DRESS HOW YOU WANT. EMBRACE YOUR DESIRES. SHOW UP EVERYWHERE AS WHO YOU REALLY ARE WITHOUT WORRIES OF JUDGMENT. YOU DESERVE IT!

DAILY AFFIRMATIONS

1. ....
2. ....
3. ....

Bonus: Read each affirmation 10x in the mirror & throughout the day for faster results.

3 PRIORITY GOALS

1. ....
2. ....
3. ....

Self Care Check

- ☐ **PHYSICAL** Rest & recharge.
- ☐ **SOCIAL** Quality conversation.
- ☐ **SPIRITUAL** Good for the soul.
- ☐ **HOUSEHOLD** Cleaning or organizing.
- ☐ **PAMPERING** Treat yourself.
- ☐ **PERSONAL** Time on a hobby.
- ☐ **EMOTIONAL** Honor feelings.
- ☐ **MENTAL** Read or learn.

MY THOUGHTS & NOTES

EVENING REFLECTIONS

DATE: .... /......... /.........

Be grateful for the limitless potential that lies within you.
—Bob Proctor proctorgallagher

GRATITUDE CHECK

TONIGHT I AM GRATEFUL FOR . . .

1. ....

2. ....

3. ....

Wellness Check

- ☐ **WORKOUT**
- ☐ **NATURE**
- ☐ **MEDITATION**
- **CAFFEINE:** ....
- ☐ **NUTRITION**
- **STEPS:** ....

WATER INTAKE:

MENTAL HEALTH CHECK

RIGHT NOW I FEEL . . . (YOU MAY CHOOSE MORE THAN ONE)

☐ HAPPY	☐ PEACEFUL	☐ PROUD
☐ LOVING	☐ CREATIVE	☐ SAD
☐ HOPEFUL	☐ STRESSED	☐ TIRED
☐ CALM	☐ ANNOYED	☐ SCARED
☐ ANGRY	☐ POSITIVE	☐ JOYFUL
☐ OVERWHELMED	☐ ANXIOUS	☐ ....

WHAT DO YOU WANT TO FOCUS ON MOST TOMORROW?

....

....

....

WINS FOR THE DAY

TODAY I ACCOMPLISHED . . .

....

....

....

....

MY THOUGHTS & NOTES

....

....

....

....

....

MORNING INTENTIONS

DATE: .... /........ /........

Ignoring our feelings never makes them go away, it just delays our pain. Let the feeling come up and then let it go. @powerofpositivity

I FEEL . . . I WANT TO FEEL ....

GRATITUDE CHECK

TODAY I AM GRATEFUL FOR . . .

1. ....
2. ....
3. ....

INSPIRE YOURSELF TODAY. MAKE A PINTEREST BOARD OF YOUR FAVORITES. PLAY AND EXPLORE NEW THINGS THAT CATCH YOUR INTEREST.

DAILY AFFIRMATIONS

1. ....
2. ....
3. ....

Bonus: Read each affirmation 10x in the mirror & throughout the day for faster results.

3 PRIORITY GOALS

1. ....
2. ....
3. ....

Self Care Check

- ☐ **PHYSICAL** Rest & recharge.
- ☐ **SOCIAL** Quality conversation.
- ☐ **SPIRITUAL** Good for the soul.
- ☐ **HOUSEHOLD** Cleaning or organizing.
- ☐ **PAMPERING** Treat yourself.
- ☐ **PERSONAL** Time on a hobby.
- ☐ **EMOTIONAL** Honor feelings.
- ☐ **MENTAL** Read or learn.

MY THOUGHTS & NOTES

EVENING REFLECTIONS

DATE: .... /........ /........

In solitude, I find my answers. —Kristen Butler @positivekristen

GRATITUDE CHECK

TONIGHT I AM GRATEFUL FOR . . .

1. ....
2. ....
3. ....

Wellness Check

- ☐ **WORKOUT**
- ☐ **NATURE**
- ☐ **MEDITATION**
- **CAFFEINE:** ....
- ☐ **NUTRITION**
- **STEPS:** ....

WATER INTAKE:

MENTAL HEALTH CHECK

RIGHT NOW I FEEL . . . (YOU MAY CHOOSE MORE THAN ONE)

- ☐ HAPPY
- ☐ LOVING
- ☐ HOPEFUL
- ☐ CALM
- ☐ ANGRY
- ☐ OVERWHELMED
- ☐ PEACEFUL
- ☐ CREATIVE
- ☐ STRESSED
- ☐ ANNOYED
- ☐ POSITIVE
- ☐ ANXIOUS
- ☐ PROUD
- ☐ SAD
- ☐ TIRED
- ☐ SCARED
- ☐ JOYFUL
- ☐ ....

WHAT DOES UNCONDITIONAL LOVE LOOK LIKE TO YOU?

WINS FOR THE DAY

TODAY I ACCOMPLISHED . . .

MY THOUGHTS & NOTES

MORNING INTENTIONS

DATE: .... /........ /........

When things go wrong, don't go with them. —Elvis Presley

I FEEL . . . I WANT TO FEEL ....

GRATITUDE CHECK

TODAY I AM GRATEFUL FOR . . .

1. ....
2. ....
3. ....

LET'S PLAY "BODY GRATITUDE". MOVE AROUND YOUR BODY, POINT TO EACH BODY PART AND SAY WHAT YOU ARE MOST GRATEFUL FOR ABOUT IT.

DAILY AFFIRMATIONS

1. ....
2. ....
3. ....

Bonus: Read each affirmation 10x in the mirror & throughout the day for faster results.

3 PRIORITY GOALS

1. ....
2. ....
3. ....

Self Care Check

- ☐ **PHYSICAL** Rest & recharge.
- ☐ **SOCIAL** Quality conversation.
- ☐ **SPIRITUAL** Good for the soul.
- ☐ **HOUSEHOLD** Cleaning or organizing.
- ☐ **PAMPERING** Treat yourself.
- ☐ **PERSONAL** Time on a hobby.
- ☐ **EMOTIONAL** Honor feelings.
- ☐ **MENTAL** Read or learn.

MY THOUGHTS & NOTES

....

....

....

....

....

EVENING REFLECTIONS

DATE: .... / .... / ....

In order to elevate ourselves and our children, we must create an intentional life. @thelaurenmagers

GRATITUDE CHECK

TONIGHT I AM GRATEFUL FOR . . .

1. ....

2. ....

3. ....

Wellness Check

- ☐ **WORKOUT**
- ☐ **NATURE**
- ☐ **MEDITATION**
- **CAFFEINE**: ....
- ☐ **NUTRITION**
- **STEPS**: ....

WATER INTAKE:

MENTAL HEALTH CHECK

RIGHT NOW I FEEL . . . (YOU MAY CHOOSE MORE THAN ONE)

- ☐ HAPPY
- ☐ LOVING
- ☐ HOPEFUL
- ☐ CALM
- ☐ ANGRY
- ☐ OVERWHELMED
- ☐ PEACEFUL
- ☐ CREATIVE
- ☐ STRESSED
- ☐ ANNOYED
- ☐ POSITIVE
- ☐ ANXIOUS
- ☐ PROUD
- ☐ SAD
- ☐ TIRED
- ☐ SCARED
- ☐ JOYFUL
- ☐ ....

I FEEL HAPPIEST WHEN . . .

WINS FOR THE DAY

TODAY I ACCOMPLISHED . . .

MY THOUGHTS & NOTES

MORNING INTENTIONS

DATE: .... /........ /........

Wake up and smile, because today can be a great day! Look for opportunities to smile and bless others. @powerofpositivity

I FEEL . . . I WANT TO FEEL ....

GRATITUDE CHECK

TODAY I AM GRATEFUL FOR . . .

1. ....
2. ....
3. ....

IT'S SO IMPORTANT TO GROUND YOURSELF DAILY. TAKE A WALK OUTSIDE, TURN ON A COLD SHOWER, DRINK A CUP OF HERBAL TEA, PET AN ANIMAL, USE AROMATHERAPY OILS.

DAILY AFFIRMATIONS

1. ....
2. ....
3. ....

Bonus: Read each affirmation 10x in the mirror & throughout the day for faster results.

3 PRIORITY GOALS

1. ....
2. ....
3. ....

Self Care Check

- ☐ **PHYSICAL** Rest & recharge.
- ☐ **SOCIAL** Quality conversation.
- ☐ **SPIRITUAL** Good for the soul.
- ☐ **HOUSEHOLD** Cleaning or organizing.
- ☐ **PAMPERING** Treat yourself.
- ☐ **PERSONAL** Time on a hobby.
- ☐ **EMOTIONAL** Honor feelings.
- ☐ **MENTAL** Read or learn.

MY THOUGHTS & NOTES

....

....

....

....

....

EVENING REFLECTIONS

DATE: .... / .... / ....

When negative energy surrounds you, stay calm. Solutions are not created any other way. —Kristen Butler @positivekristen

GRATITUDE CHECK

TONIGHT I AM GRATEFUL FOR . . .

1. ....
2. ....
3. ....

Wellness Check

- ☐ **WORKOUT**
- ☐ **NATURE**
- ☐ **MEDITATION**
- **CAFFEINE:** ....
- ☐ **NUTRITION**
- **STEPS:** ....

WATER INTAKE:

MENTAL HEALTH CHECK

RIGHT NOW I FEEL . . . (YOU MAY CHOOSE MORE THAN ONE)

☐ HAPPY	☐ PEACEFUL	☐ PROUD
☐ LOVING	☐ CREATIVE	☐ SAD
☐ HOPEFUL	☐ STRESSED	☐ TIRED
☐ CALM	☐ ANNOYED	☐ SCARED
☐ ANGRY	☐ POSITIVE	☐ JOYFUL
☐ OVERWHELMED	☐ ANXIOUS	☐ ....

WHAT DO YOU WANT YOUR LEGACY TO BE?

....

....

....

WINS FOR THE DAY

TODAY I ACCOMPLISHED . . .

....

....

....

....

MY THOUGHTS & NOTES

....

....

....

....

....

MORNING INTENTIONS

DATE: .... /........ /........

Positive thoughts in the morning can guide the direction of your day. Be aware of your self-talk and redirect negativity. @powerofpositivity

I FEEL . . . I WANT TO FEEL ....

GRATITUDE CHECK

TODAY I AM GRATEFUL FOR . . .

1. ....
2. ....
3. ....

DO YOU FEEL HEALTHY? IF YOU ANSWERED NO, WRITE A NEW DAILY AFFIRMATION ABOUT HAVING A HEALTHY BODY.

DAILY AFFIRMATIONS

1. ....
2. ....
3. ....

Bonus: Read each affirmation 10x in the mirror & throughout the day for faster results.

3 PRIORITY GOALS

1. ....
2. ....
3. ....

Self Care Check

- ☐ **PHYSICAL** Rest & recharge.
- ☐ **SOCIAL** Quality conversation.
- ☐ **SPIRITUAL** Good for the soul.
- ☐ **HOUSEHOLD** Cleaning or organizing.
- ☐ **PAMPERING** Treat yourself.
- ☐ **PERSONAL** Time on a hobby.
- ☐ **EMOTIONAL** Honor feelings.
- ☐ **MENTAL** Read or learn.

MY THOUGHTS & NOTES

....

....

....

....

....

EVENING REFLECTIONS

DATE: .... /........ /........

Stay positive even when it feels like things are falling apart.
@powerofpositivity

GRATITUDE CHECK

TONIGHT I AM GRATEFUL FOR . . .

1. ....

2. ....

3. ....

Wellness Check

- ☐ **WORKOUT**
- ☐ **NATURE**
- ☐ **MEDITATION**
- **CAFFEINE:** ....
- ☐ **NUTRITION**
- **STEPS:** ....

WATER INTAKE:

MENTAL HEALTH CHECK

RIGHT NOW I FEEL . . . (YOU MAY CHOOSE MORE THAN ONE)

☐ HAPPY	☐ PEACEFUL	☐ PROUD
☐ LOVING	☐ CREATIVE	☐ SAD
☐ HOPEFUL	☐ STRESSED	☐ TIRED
☐ CALM	☐ ANNOYED	☐ SCARED
☐ ANGRY	☐ POSITIVE	☐ JOYFUL
☐ OVERWHELMED	☐ ANXIOUS	☐ ....

DO YOU COMPLIMENT YOURSELF? WHAT DO YOU SAY?

....

....

....

WINS FOR THE DAY

TODAY I ACCOMPLISHED . . .

....

....

....

....

MY THOUGHTS & NOTES

....

....

....

....

....

MORNING INTENTIONS

DATE: .... /........ /........

Let no man pull you so low as to hate him. —Martin Luther King Jr.

I FEEL . . . I WANT TO FEEL ....

GRATITUDE CHECK

TODAY I AM GRATEFUL FOR . . .

1. ....
2. ....
3. ....

DO YOU HAVE HOPE FOR YOUR FUTURE? IF THINGS FEEL ROCKY, SIT HERE RIGHT NOW AND PRAY OR SEND POSITIVE VIBES FOR OPPORTUNITIES THAT SERVE YOUR HIGHEST GOOD.

DAILY AFFIRMATIONS

1. ....
2. ....
3. ....

Bonus: Read each affirmation 10x in the mirror & throughout the day for faster results.

3 PRIORITY GOALS

1. ....
2. ....
3. ....

Self Care Check

- ☐ **PHYSICAL** Rest & recharge.
- ☐ **SOCIAL** Quality conversation.
- ☐ **SPIRITUAL** Good for the soul.
- ☐ **HOUSEHOLD** Cleaning or organizing.
- ☐ **PAMPERING** Treat yourself.
- ☐ **PERSONAL** Time on a hobby.
- ☐ **EMOTIONAL** Honor feelings.
- ☐ **MENTAL** Read or learn.

MY THOUGHTS & NOTES

....

....

....

....

....

EVENING REFLECTIONS

DATE: .... / .... / ....

Always remember that your present situation is not your final destination. The best is yet to come. —Zig Ziglar

---

GRATITUDE CHECK

TONIGHT I AM GRATEFUL FOR . . .

1. ....

2. ....

3. ....

Wellness Check

- ☐ **WORKOUT**
- ☐ **NATURE**
- ☐ **MEDITATION**
- **CAFFEINE:** ....
- ☐ **NUTRITION**
- **STEPS:** ....

WATER INTAKE:

MENTAL HEALTH CHECK

RIGHT NOW I FEEL . . . (YOU MAY CHOOSE MORE THAN ONE)

☐ HAPPY	☐ PEACEFUL	☐ PROUD
☐ LOVING	☐ CREATIVE	☐ SAD
☐ HOPEFUL	☐ STRESSED	☐ TIRED
☐ CALM	☐ ANNOYED	☐ SCARED
☐ ANGRY	☐ POSITIVE	☐ JOYFUL
☐ OVERWHELMED	☐ ANXIOUS	☐ ....

I'M PROUD OF MYSELF TODAY BECAUSE . . .

....

....

....

WINS FOR THE DAY

TODAY I ACCOMPLISHED . . .

....

....

....

....

MY THOUGHTS & NOTES

....

....

....

....

....

MORNING INTENTIONS

DATE: .... /........ /........

Do not go where the path may lead, go instead where there is no path and leave a trail. —Ralph Waldo Emerson

I FEEL . . . I WANT TO FEEL ....

GRATITUDE CHECK

TODAY I AM GRATEFUL FOR . . .

1. ....
2. ....
3. ....

REMEMBER, NOT ALL THOUGHTS ARE FACTS. WHAT LIMITING BELIEFS CAN YOU RELEASE TODAY?

DAILY AFFIRMATIONS

1. ....
2. ....
3. ....

Bonus: Read each affirmation 10x in the mirror & throughout the day for faster results.

3 PRIORITY GOALS

1. ....
2. ....
3. ....

Self Care Check

- ☐ **PHYSICAL** Rest & recharge.
- ☐ **SOCIAL** Quality conversation.
- ☐ **SPIRITUAL** Good for the soul.
- ☐ **HOUSEHOLD** Cleaning or organizing.
- ☐ **PAMPERING** Treat yourself.
- ☐ **PERSONAL** Time on a hobby.
- ☐ **EMOTIONAL** Honor feelings.
- ☐ **MENTAL** Read or learn.

MY THOUGHTS & NOTES

....

....

....

....

....

EVENING REFLECTIONS

DATE: .... /......... /.........

Don't judge. You don't know what kind of storms someone has just walked through. —Kristen Butler @positivekristen

GRATITUDE CHECK

TONIGHT I AM GRATEFUL FOR . . .

1. ....

2. ....

3. ....

Wellness Check

☐ WORKOUT ☐ NATURE

☐ MEDITATION CAFFEINE: ....

☐ NUTRITION STEPS: ....

WATER INTAKE:

MENTAL HEALTH CHECK

RIGHT NOW I FEEL . . . (YOU MAY CHOOSE MORE THAN ONE)

☐ HAPPY	☐ PEACEFUL	☐ PROUD
☐ LOVING	☐ CREATIVE	☐ SAD
☐ HOPEFUL	☐ STRESSED	☐ TIRED
☐ CALM	☐ ANNOYED	☐ SCARED
☐ ANGRY	☐ POSITIVE	☐ JOYFUL
☐ OVERWHELMED	☐ ANXIOUS	☐ ....

ARE YOU GETTING ENOUGH SLEEP EVERY NIGHT? IF NOT, HOW CAN YOU IMPROVE IT?

....

....

....

WINS FOR THE DAY

TODAY I ACCOMPLISHED . . .

....

....

....

....

MY THOUGHTS & NOTES

....

....

....

....

....

MORNING INTENTIONS

DATE: .... /........ /........

A mind filled with worry does not release tomorrow's problems, only faith can do that. @powerofpositivity

I FEEL . . . I WANT TO FEEL ....

GRATITUDE CHECK

TODAY I AM GRATEFUL FOR . . .

1. ....
2. ....
3. ....

NEGATIVE THOUGHTS HAPPEN, BUT WHERE DO YOURS PRIMARILY COME FROM? OTHERS? NEGATIVE SELF-TALK? TRAUMA? HOW CAN YOU FLIP THE SCRIPT?

DAILY AFFIRMATIONS

1. ....
2. ....
3. ....

Bonus: Read each affirmation 10x in the mirror & throughout the day for faster results.

3 PRIORITY GOALS

1. ....
2. ....
3. ....

Self Care Check

- ☐ **PHYSICAL** Rest & recharge.
- ☐ **SOCIAL** Quality conversation.
- ☐ **SPIRITUAL** Good for the soul.
- ☐ **HOUSEHOLD** Cleaning or organizing.
- ☐ **PAMPERING** Treat yourself.
- ☐ **PERSONAL** Time on a hobby.
- ☐ **EMOTIONAL** Honor feelings.
- ☐ **MENTAL** Read or learn.

MY THOUGHTS & NOTES

....

....

....

....

....

EVENING REFLECTIONS

DATE: .... /........ /........

The more you lose yourself in something bigger than yourself, the more energy you will have. —Norman Vincent Peale

GRATITUDE CHECK

TONIGHT I AM GRATEFUL FOR . . .

1. ....

2. ....

3. ....

Wellness Check

- ☐ **WORKOUT**
- ☐ **NATURE**
- ☐ **MEDITATION**
- **CAFFEINE:** ....
- ☐ **NUTRITION**
- **STEPS:** ....

WATER INTAKE:

MENTAL HEALTH CHECK

RIGHT NOW I FEEL . . . (YOU MAY CHOOSE MORE THAN ONE)

☐ HAPPY	☐ PEACEFUL	☐ PROUD
☐ LOVING	☐ CREATIVE	☐ SAD
☐ HOPEFUL	☐ STRESSED	☐ TIRED
☐ CALM	☐ ANNOYED	☐ SCARED
☐ ANGRY	☐ POSITIVE	☐ JOYFUL
☐ OVERWHELMED	☐ ANXIOUS	☐ ....

DO YOU FEEL LIKE YOU'RE IN A GOOD PLACE WITH YOUR CAREER? WHY?

....

....

....

WINS FOR THE DAY

TODAY I ACCOMPLISHED . . .

....

....

....

....

MY THOUGHTS & NOTES

....

....

....

....

....

MORNING INTENTIONS

DATE: .... /........ /........

Failure is feedback. Every time something doesn't go your way, find the lesson and move forward. You will always find success this way. lewishowes

I FEEL . . . I WANT TO FEEL ....

GRATITUDE CHECK

TODAY I AM GRATEFUL FOR . . .

1. ....
2. ....
3. ....

CHECK IN WITH YOUR BODY RIGHT NOW. WHAT ARE SOME SENSATIONS YOU ARE FEELING? DON'T JUDGE, JUST BE MINDFUL AND CHECK IN LIKE THIS MORE OFTEN.

DAILY AFFIRMATIONS

1. ....
2. ....
3. ....

Bonus: Read each affirmation 10x in the mirror & throughout the day for faster results.

3 PRIORITY GOALS

1. ....
2. ....
3. ....

Self Care Check

- ☐ **PHYSICAL** Rest & recharge.
- ☐ **SOCIAL** Quality conversation.
- ☐ **SPIRITUAL** Good for the soul.
- ☐ **HOUSEHOLD** Cleaning or organizing.
- ☐ **PAMPERING** Treat yourself.
- ☐ **PERSONAL** Time on a hobby.
- ☐ **EMOTIONAL** Honor feelings.
- ☐ **MENTAL** Read or learn.

MY THOUGHTS & NOTES

....

....

....

....

....

EVENING REFLECTIONS

DATE: .... / .... / ....

Stop, think of all the good moments that happened today and fall asleep tonight with love in your heart and peace in your soul. @powerofpositivity

GRATITUDE CHECK

TONIGHT I AM GRATEFUL FOR . . .

1. ....

2. ....

3. ....

Wellness Check

- ☐ **WORKOUT**
- ☐ **NATURE**
- ☐ **MEDITATION**
- **CAFFEINE:** ....
- ☐ **NUTRITION**
- **STEPS:** ....

WATER INTAKE:

MENTAL HEALTH CHECK

RIGHT NOW I FEEL . . . (YOU MAY CHOOSE MORE THAN ONE)

- ☐ HAPPY
- ☐ LOVING
- ☐ HOPEFUL
- ☐ CALM
- ☐ ANGRY
- ☐ OVERWHELMED
- ☐ PEACEFUL
- ☐ CREATIVE
- ☐ STRESSED
- ☐ ANNOYED
- ☐ POSITIVE
- ☐ ANXIOUS
- ☐ PROUD
- ☐ SAD
- ☐ TIRED
- ☐ SCARED
- ☐ JOYFUL
- ☐ ....

DO YOU FEEL LIKE YOU ARE LIVING YOUR LIFE PURPOSE? WHAT DOES THAT LOOK LIKE?

....

....

....

WINS FOR THE DAY

TODAY I ACCOMPLISHED . . .

....

....

....

....

MY THOUGHTS & NOTES

....

....

....

....

....

MORNING INTENTIONS

DATE: .... /........ /........

Be miserable or motivate yourself. Whatever has to be done, it's always your choice. —Wayne Dyer

---

I FEEL . . . I WANT TO FEEL ....

GRATITUDE CHECK

TODAY I AM GRATEFUL FOR . . .

1. ....
2. ....
3. ....

DO YOU TAKE NAPS? WOULD YOU CONSIDER TAKING ONE TODAY OR THIS WEEK? DON'T FEEL BAD FOR TAKING TIME FOR YOURSELF. REST HEALS AND RECHARGES YOU.

DAILY AFFIRMATIONS

1. ....
2. ....
3. ....

Bonus: Read each affirmation 10x in the mirror & throughout the day for faster results.

3 PRIORITY GOALS

1. ....
2. ....
3. ....

Self Care Check

- ☐ **PHYSICAL** Rest & recharge.
- ☐ **SOCIAL** Quality conversation.
- ☐ **SPIRITUAL** Good for the soul.
- ☐ **HOUSEHOLD** Cleaning or organizing.
- ☐ **PAMPERING** Treat yourself.
- ☐ **PERSONAL** Time on a hobby.
- ☐ **EMOTIONAL** Honor feelings.
- ☐ **MENTAL** Read or learn.

MY THOUGHTS & NOTES

....

....

....

....

....

EVENING REFLECTIONS

DATE: .... /........ /........

You can never change your life or move forward if you keep feeding your mind with old thoughts. @ClionaOhara

---

GRATITUDE CHECK

TONIGHT I AM GRATEFUL FOR . . .

1. ....

2. ....

3. ....

Wellness Check

- ☐ **WORKOUT**
- ☐ **NATURE**
- ☐ **MEDITATION**
- **CAFFEINE:** ....
- ☐ **NUTRITION**
- **STEPS:** ....

WATER INTAKE:

MENTAL HEALTH CHECK

RIGHT NOW I FEEL . . . (YOU MAY CHOOSE MORE THAN ONE)

☐ HAPPY	☐ PEACEFUL	☐ PROUD
☐ LOVING	☐ CREATIVE	☐ SAD
☐ HOPEFUL	☐ STRESSED	☐ TIRED
☐ CALM	☐ ANNOYED	☐ SCARED
☐ ANGRY	☐ POSITIVE	☐ JOYFUL
☐ OVERWHELMED	☐ ANXIOUS	☐ ....

WHAT ARE YOUR FAVORITE SELF-CARE ACTIVITIES? WHAT'S A NEW ONE YOU WANT TO ADD?

....

....

....

WINS FOR THE DAY

TODAY I ACCOMPLISHED . . .

....

....

....

....

MY THOUGHTS & NOTES

....

....

....

....

....

MORNING INTENTIONS

DATE: .... / .... / ....

Instead of planning for the worst case scenario and feeding your anxiety, how about expecting the best-case scenario and restoring your peace. @positivekristen

I FEEL . . . I WANT TO FEEL ....

GRATITUDE CHECK

TODAY I AM GRATEFUL FOR . . .

1. ....
2. ....
3. ....

HOW OFTEN DO YOU READ SELF-HELP BOOKS? EVEN 20 MINUTES A DAY CAN GUIDE YOU AND CHANGE YOUR LIFE FOR THE BETTER.

DAILY AFFIRMATIONS

1. ....
2. ....
3. ....

Bonus: Read each affirmation 10x in the mirror & throughout the day for faster results.

3 PRIORITY GOALS

1. ....
2. ....
3. ....

Self Care Check

- ☐ **PHYSICAL** Rest & recharge.
- ☐ **SOCIAL** Quality conversation.
- ☐ **SPIRITUAL** Good for the soul.
- ☐ **HOUSEHOLD** Cleaning or organizing.
- ☐ **PAMPERING** Treat yourself.
- ☐ **PERSONAL** Time on a hobby.
- ☐ **EMOTIONAL** Honor feelings.
- ☐ **MENTAL** Read or learn.

MY THOUGHTS & NOTES

....

....

....

....

....

EVENING REFLECTIONS

DATE: .... / .... / ....

Four things for success: work and pray, think and believe.
—Norman Vincent Peale

GRATITUDE CHECK

TONIGHT I AM GRATEFUL FOR . . .

1. ....

2. ....

3. ....

Wellness Check

- ☐ WORKOUT
- ☐ NATURE
- ☐ MEDITATION
- CAFFEINE: ....
- ☐ NUTRITION
- STEPS: ....

WATER INTAKE:

MENTAL HEALTH CHECK

RIGHT NOW I FEEL . . . (YOU MAY CHOOSE MORE THAN ONE)

☐ HAPPY	☐ PEACEFUL	☐ PROUD
☐ LOVING	☐ CREATIVE	☐ SAD
☐ HOPEFUL	☐ STRESSED	☐ TIRED
☐ CALM	☐ ANNOYED	☐ SCARED
☐ ANGRY	☐ POSITIVE	☐ JOYFUL
☐ OVERWHELMED	☐ ANXIOUS	☐ ....

DO YOU OVERTHINK? IF SO, ABOUT WHAT?

WINS FOR THE DAY

TODAY I ACCOMPLISHED . . .

MY THOUGHTS & NOTES

MORNING INTENTIONS

DATE: .... / .... / ....

Get real with yourself. Take control of your mind. Negative thoughts will never give you a positive life. @powerofpositivity

I FEEL . . . I WANT TO FEEL ....

GRATITUDE CHECK

TODAY I AM GRATEFUL FOR . . .

1. ....
2. ....
3. ....

ARE YOU ON TRACK WITH YOUR GOALS? IF YOU ANSWERED NO, REVISIT THE AFFIRMATIONS SECTION AND CREATE A NEW ONE ABOUT ACHIEVING GOALS.

DAILY AFFIRMATIONS

1. ....
2. ....
3. ....

Bonus: Read each affirmation 10x in the mirror & throughout the day for faster results.

3 PRIORITY GOALS

1. ....
2. ....
3. ....

Self Care Check

- ☐ **PHYSICAL** Rest & recharge.
- ☐ **SOCIAL** Quality conversation.
- ☐ **SPIRITUAL** Good for the soul.
- ☐ **HOUSEHOLD** Cleaning or organizing.
- ☐ **PAMPERING** Treat yourself.
- ☐ **PERSONAL** Time on a hobby.
- ☐ **EMOTIONAL** Honor feelings.
- ☐ **MENTAL** Read or learn.

MY THOUGHTS & NOTES

....

EVENING REFLECTIONS

DATE: .... /......... /.........

Keep your head and your heart going in the right direction and you will not have to worry about your feet. —African Proverb

GRATITUDE CHECK

TONIGHT I AM GRATEFUL FOR . . .

1. ....

2. ....

3. ....

Wellness Check

☐ **WORKOUT** ☐ **NATURE**

☐ **MEDITATION** **CAFFEINE:** ....

☐ **NUTRITION** **STEPS:** ....

WATER INTAKE:

MENTAL HEALTH CHECK

RIGHT NOW I FEEL . . . (YOU MAY CHOOSE MORE THAN ONE)

☐ HAPPY
☐ LOVING
☐ HOPEFUL
☐ CALM
☐ ANGRY
☐ OVERWHELMED
☐ PEACEFUL
☐ CREATIVE
☐ STRESSED
☐ ANNOYED
☐ POSITIVE
☐ ANXIOUS
☐ PROUD
☐ SAD
☐ TIRED
☐ SCARED
☐ JOYFUL
☐ ....

HOW CAN YOU ADD MORE LAUGHTER INTO YOUR DAY?

....

....

....

WINS FOR THE DAY

TODAY I ACCOMPLISHED . . .

....

....

....

....

MY THOUGHTS & NOTES

....

....

....

....

....

MORNING INTENTIONS

DATE: .... / .... / ....

Sometimes all you can do is keep your head up, stay strong, let go, and move on.

I FEEL . . . I WANT TO FEEL ....

GRATITUDE CHECK

TODAY I AM GRATEFUL FOR . . .

1. ....
2. ....
3. ....

DESIGN AN INSPIRATIONAL COLLAGE FULL OF IMAGES THAT MAKE YOU HAPPY, AND DISPLAY IT NEAR YOUR DESK.

DAILY AFFIRMATIONS

1. ....
2. ....
3. ....

Bonus: Read each affirmation 10x in the mirror & throughout the day for faster results.

3 PRIORITY GOALS

1. ....
2. ....
3. ....

Self Care Check

- ☐ **PHYSICAL** Rest & recharge.
- ☐ **SOCIAL** Quality conversation.
- ☐ **SPIRITUAL** Good for the soul.
- ☐ **HOUSEHOLD** Cleaning or organizing.
- ☐ **PAMPERING** Treat yourself.
- ☐ **PERSONAL** Time on a hobby.
- ☐ **EMOTIONAL** Honor feelings.
- ☐ **MENTAL** Read or learn.

MY THOUGHTS & NOTES

....

EVENING REFLECTIONS

DATE: .... / .... / ....

When you continuously spread positive vibes, Karma is naturally rigged in your favor. Life loves authenticity and consistency. —Kristen Butler @positivekristen

GRATITUDE CHECK

TONIGHT I AM GRATEFUL FOR . . .

1. ....

2. ....

3. ....

Wellness Check

- ☐ **WORKOUT**
- ☐ **NATURE**
- ☐ **MEDITATION**
- **CAFFEINE:** ....
- ☐ **NUTRITION**
- **STEPS:** ....

WATER INTAKE:

MENTAL HEALTH CHECK

RIGHT NOW I FEEL . . . (YOU MAY CHOOSE MORE THAN ONE)

☐ HAPPY	☐ PEACEFUL	☐ PROUD
☐ LOVING	☐ CREATIVE	☐ SAD
☐ HOPEFUL	☐ STRESSED	☐ TIRED
☐ CALM	☐ ANNOYED	☐ SCARED
☐ ANGRY	☐ POSITIVE	☐ JOYFUL
☐ OVERWHELMED	☐ ANXIOUS	☐ ....

WRITE ABOUT A TIME WHEN YOU WERE RESILIENT . . .

....

....

....

WINS FOR THE DAY

TODAY I ACCOMPLISHED . . .

....

....

....

....

MY THOUGHTS & NOTES

....

....

....

....

....

MORNING INTENTIONS

DATE: .... / .... / ....

Challenges can't stop you. People can't stop you. Time can't stop you. Your own negative thoughts can. Stay positive. —Kristen Butler @positivekristen

I FEEL . . . I WANT TO FEEL ....

GRATITUDE CHECK

TODAY I AM GRATEFUL FOR . . .

1. ....
2. ....
3. ....

SOMETIMES SILENCE IS BETTER THAN ANY EXPLANATION. YOU DON'T OWE ANYONE ONE. USE YOUR INTUITION AND STAY SILENT DURING AN ARGUMENT. STOP IT IN ITS TRACKS.

DAILY AFFIRMATIONS

1. ....
2. ....
3. ....

Bonus: Read each affirmation 10x in the mirror & throughout the day for faster results.

3 PRIORITY GOALS

1. ....
2. ....
3. ....

Self Care Check

- ☐ **PHYSICAL** Rest & recharge.
- ☐ **SOCIAL** Quality conversation.
- ☐ **SPIRITUAL** Good for the soul.
- ☐ **HOUSEHOLD** Cleaning or organizing.
- ☐ **PAMPERING** Treat yourself.
- ☐ **PERSONAL** Time on a hobby.
- ☐ **EMOTIONAL** Honor feelings.
- ☐ **MENTAL** Read or learn.

MY THOUGHTS & NOTES

EVENING REFLECTIONS

DATE: .... /........ /........

A positive outlook may not solve all of your problems, but it will give you a happier life. @powerofpositivity

---

GRATITUDE CHECK

TONIGHT I AM GRATEFUL FOR . . .

1. ....
2. ....
3. ....

Wellness Check

- ☐ **WORKOUT**
- ☐ **NATURE**
- ☐ **MEDITATION**
- **CAFFEINE:** ....
- ☐ **NUTRITION**
- **STEPS:** ....

WATER INTAKE:

MENTAL HEALTH CHECK

RIGHT NOW I FEEL . . . (YOU MAY CHOOSE MORE THAN ONE)

☐ HAPPY	☐ PEACEFUL	☐ PROUD
☐ LOVING	☐ CREATIVE	☐ SAD
☐ HOPEFUL	☐ STRESSED	☐ TIRED
☐ CALM	☐ ANNOYED	☐ SCARED
☐ ANGRY	☐ POSITIVE	☐ JOYFUL
☐ OVERWHELMED	☐ ANXIOUS	☐ ....

WRITE DOWN 5 THINGS YOUR INNER CRITIC SAYS TO YOU. WHAT CAN YOU SAY TO COUNTER THAT?

....

....

....

WINS FOR THE DAY

TODAY I ACCOMPLISHED . . .

....

....

....

....

MY THOUGHTS & NOTES

....

....

....

....

....

MORNING INTENTIONS

DATE: .... /......... /.........

Before you try to fix someone else's vibe, make sure you're not killing your own in the process. Protect your own energy first. —Vex King @vexking

I FEEL . . . I WANT TO FEEL ....

GRATITUDE CHECK

TODAY I AM GRATEFUL FOR . . .

1. ....
2. ....
3. ....

DISTRACTIONS KEEP YOU FROM YOUR GOALS. NEXT TIME YOU ARE TRYING TO CONCENTRATE, TURN OFF THE TV, PUT YOUR PHONE ON SILENT, DON'T PLAY ANY MUSIC. STAY FOCUSED UNTIL YOU COMPLETE IT.

DAILY AFFIRMATIONS

1. ....
2. ....
3. ....

Bonus: Read each affirmation 10x in the mirror & throughout the day for faster results.

3 PRIORITY GOALS

1. ....
2. ....
3. ....

Self Care Check

- ☐ **PHYSICAL** Rest & recharge.
- ☐ **SOCIAL** Quality conversation.
- ☐ **SPIRITUAL** Good for the soul.
- ☐ **HOUSEHOLD** Cleaning or organizing.
- ☐ **PAMPERING** Treat yourself.
- ☐ **PERSONAL** Time on a hobby.
- ☐ **EMOTIONAL** Honor feelings.
- ☐ **MENTAL** Read or learn.

MY THOUGHTS & NOTES

....

....

....

....

....

EVENING REFLECTIONS

DATE: .... /........ /........

All the answers to questions you'll ever ask, can be found within you. Just simply ask and wait. —Eugene Butler

GRATITUDE CHECK

TONIGHT I AM GRATEFUL FOR . . .

1. ....

2. ....

3. ....

Wellness Check

☐ **WORKOUT** ☐ **NATURE**

☐ **MEDITATION** **CAFFEINE:** ....

☐ **NUTRITION** **STEPS:** ....

WATER INTAKE:

MENTAL HEALTH CHECK

RIGHT NOW I FEEL . . . (YOU MAY CHOOSE MORE THAN ONE)

☐ HAPPY	☐ PEACEFUL	☐ PROUD
☐ LOVING	☐ CREATIVE	☐ SAD
☐ HOPEFUL	☐ STRESSED	☐ TIRED
☐ CALM	☐ ANNOYED	☐ SCARED
☐ ANGRY	☐ POSITIVE	☐ JOYFUL
☐ OVERWHELMED	☐ ANXIOUS	☐ ....

IF YOU COULD GIVE ANYONE A PIECE OF ADVICE TO GET THROUGH THEIR DAY, WHAT WOULD IT BE?

WINS FOR THE DAY

TODAY I ACCOMPLISHED . . .

MY THOUGHTS & NOTES

MORNING INTENTIONS

DATE: .... /........ /........

Nothing will slow your progress like negative thinking. Stay positive, no matter what is happening around you. It makes all the difference. @powerofpositivity

---

I FEEL . . . I WANT TO FEEL ....

GRATITUDE CHECK

TODAY I AM GRATEFUL FOR . . .

1. ....
2. ....
3. ....

DO YOU JUDGE YOURSELF OR OTHERS? HOW CAN YOU PRACTICE MORE COMPASSION AND RELEASE JUDGMENTAL IMPULSES AS THEY ARISE?

DAILY AFFIRMATIONS

1. ....
2. ....
3. ....

Bonus: Read each affirmation 10x in the mirror & throughout the day for faster results.

3 PRIORITY GOALS

1. ....
2. ....
3. ....

Self Care Check

- ☐ **PHYSICAL** Rest & recharge.
- ☐ **SOCIAL** Quality conversation.
- ☐ **SPIRITUAL** Good for the soul.
- ☐ **HOUSEHOLD** Cleaning or organizing.
- ☐ **PAMPERING** Treat yourself.
- ☐ **PERSONAL** Time on a hobby.
- ☐ **EMOTIONAL** Honor feelings.
- ☐ **MENTAL** Read or learn.

MY THOUGHTS & NOTES

....

....

....

....

....

EVENING REFLECTIONS

DATE: .... /........ /........

Be grateful you have a safe, secure place to sleep tonight. Some people don't have that luxury. —Kristen Butler @positivekristen

GRATITUDE CHECK

TONIGHT I AM GRATEFUL FOR . . .

1. ....

2. ....

3. ....

Wellness Check

☐ WORKOUT ☐ NATURE

☐ MEDITATION CAFFEINE: ....

☐ NUTRITION STEPS: ....

WATER INTAKE:

MENTAL HEALTH CHECK

RIGHT NOW I FEEL . . . (YOU MAY CHOOSE MORE THAN ONE)

☐ HAPPY	☐ PEACEFUL	☐ PROUD
☐ LOVING	☐ CREATIVE	☐ SAD
☐ HOPEFUL	☐ STRESSED	☐ TIRED
☐ CALM	☐ ANNOYED	☐ SCARED
☐ ANGRY	☐ POSITIVE	☐ JOYFUL
☐ OVERWHELMED	☐ ANXIOUS	☐ ....

DO YOU LIVE BY ANY PIECE OF ADVICE OR MOTTO?

....

....

....

WINS FOR THE DAY

TODAY I ACCOMPLISHED . . .

....

....

....

....

MY THOUGHTS & NOTES

....

....

....

....

....

MORNING INTENTIONS

DATE: .... /........ /........

Live in such a way that if someone should speak badly of you, no one would believe it. —Zig Ziglar

I FEEL . . . I WANT TO FEEL ....

GRATITUDE CHECK

TODAY I AM GRATEFUL FOR . . .

1. ....
2. ....
3. ....

HOW DO YOU FEEL AFTER 60 DAYS OF CONSISTENT DAILY CHECK-INS? FEEL THE FEELING OF ACCOMPLISHMENT. CELEBRATE. YOU'RE AMAZING. WELL DONE!

DAILY AFFIRMATIONS

1. ....
2. ....
3. ....

Bonus: Read each affirmation 10x in the mirror & throughout the day for faster results.

3 PRIORITY GOALS

1. ....
2. ....
3. ....

Self Care Check

- ☐ **PHYSICAL** Rest & recharge.
- ☐ **SOCIAL** Quality conversation.
- ☐ **SPIRITUAL** Good for the soul.
- ☐ **HOUSEHOLD** Cleaning or organizing.
- ☐ **PAMPERING** Treat yourself.
- ☐ **PERSONAL** Time on a hobby.
- ☐ **EMOTIONAL** Honor feelings.
- ☐ **MENTAL** Read or learn.

MY THOUGHTS & NOTES

....

....

....

....

....

EVENING REFLECTIONS

DATE: .... / .... / ....

Don't copy the behavior and customs of this world, but let God transform you into a new person by changing the way you think. —Romans 12:2

GRATITUDE CHECK

TONIGHT I AM GRATEFUL FOR . . .

1. ....

2. ....

3. ....

Wellness Check

- ☐ **WORKOUT**
- ☐ **NATURE**
- ☐ **MEDITATION**
- **CAFFEINE:** ....
- ☐ **NUTRITION**
- **STEPS:** ....

WATER INTAKE:

MENTAL HEALTH CHECK

RIGHT NOW I FEEL . . . (YOU MAY CHOOSE MORE THAN ONE)

☐ HAPPY	☐ PEACEFUL	☐ PROUD
☐ LOVING	☐ CREATIVE	☐ SAD
☐ HOPEFUL	☐ STRESSED	☐ TIRED
☐ CALM	☐ ANNOYED	☐ SCARED
☐ ANGRY	☐ POSITIVE	☐ JOYFUL
☐ OVERWHELMED	☐ ANXIOUS	☐ ....

WHO ARE TWO PEOPLE THAT YOU'RE EXTRA GRATEFUL FOR TODAY?

....

....

....

WINS FOR THE DAY

TODAY I ACCOMPLISHED . . .

....

....

....

....

MY THOUGHTS & NOTES

....

....

....

....

....

60 Day Reflection

Has my life changed in a positive way?

✓ ✗

WHAT HAVE I LEARNED IN THE PAST 60 DAYS?

WHAT NEW HABITS HAVE I ACQUIRED?

60 Day Reflection

Is journaling a new habit I enjoy?

✓ ✗

WHAT WERE THE BIGGEST CHALLENGES I HAD TO OVERCOME?

WHAT ARE MY NEXT STEPS?

My Final Thoughts

My Final Thoughts

My Final Thoughts

My Final Thoughts

My Final Thoughts

My Final Thoughts

My Final Thoughts

My Final Thoughts

My Final Thoughts

My Final Thoughts

My Final Thoughts

My Final Thoughts

My Final Thoughts

My Final Thoughts

My Final Thoughts

My Final Thoughts

Acknowledgments

This journal is dedicated to the Power of Positivity community, my amazing, encouraging team behind the scenes, my incredible friends and supporters, and my beautiful daughters. Thank you for remaining so patient and encouraging as I spent months immersed in bringing this creation to life. Thank you for believing in me and being there for me every step of the way.

Everyone's support has been so phenomenal. From the bottom of my heart, I am genuinely so, so grateful. Special acknowledgments to these amazing souls who were pivotal pieces in creating this journal: Dimitra Jhugroo, Stephanie Wallace, Ellie Shoja, Lakeisha Ethans, Chris Butler, Marites Bautista, Angelica Medrano, Rupa Limbu, Deborah Tayloe, Branislav Aleksoski, Cliona O'Hara, and Lewis Howes.

This journal is also dedicated to YOU. I am grateful for your support. Whether we have been connected for a long time or now through this journal, thank you! As you read the pages of this book and begin taking action daily, may it be a stepping stone towards living the fullest, most positive expression of who you really are. Thank you for being on this journey with me. Let's stay connected. We are in this together; let's do this!

About the Author

Kristen Butler is an entrepreneur, leader, writer, and visionary in personal development with a huge heart and captivating authenticity. Her mission is to uplift the planet! She is the founder and CEO of Power of Positivity. Started in 2009, today, her brands have a collective global audience of over 50 million and an amazingly talented team behind the scenes. Her success can be attributed to her passion and tenacity to help others, her experience and knowledge in social media since 1998, her love for writing, and her business and journalism skills.

She passionately started Power of Positivity after completely transforming her life from rock bottom using the power of positive thinking. She was so astonished by the results of her research and mindset implementation that she felt her life's purpose was (and still is) to help others improve their lives. Kristen not only contributes her transformation to a positive mindset but her relationship with God and an active, plant-based lifestyle.